Before Birth and Beyond Death

Karl König with his children Bernward Christof and Clara Renate, Pilgramshain 1935.

Before Birth and Beyond Death

The Transformation of the Human Being

Karl König

Floris Books

This book is dedicated to Renate Sleigh (née König, born December 3, 1930). She died July 3 2020, during the eightieth anniversary year of Camphill in Camphill Village Western Cape, South Africa. Karl König had asked her to go with a small group of co-workers to pioneer the work of Camphill in South Africa in 1957.

Karl König Archive Publication, Vol. 20
Subject: Anthroposophy
Edited by Richard Steel and Michael Bruhn

Series editor: Richard Steel

Karl König's collected works are issued by
the Karl König Archive, Aberdeen

First published in English by Floris Books in 2021
© 2021 Trustees of the Karl König Archives

All rights reserved. No part of this publication may
be reproduced without the prior permission of
Floris Books, Edinburgh
www.florisbooks.co.uk

British Library CIP Data available
ISBN 978-178250-719-2
Printed and bound in Great Britain by Bell & Bain, Ltd

Floris Books supports sustainable forest management by printing this book on materials made from wood that comes from responsible sources and reclaimed material

Contents

Introduction *by Michael Bruhn* — 7

I About Those Who Have Died
1. The Gate of Birth and the Gate of Death — 19
2. Bridges to Those who Have Died — 31
3. The Path Beyond Death — 44

II Poems
The Death of Adalbert Stifter — 57
Transformation — 64

III Birth and Death
4. The Experience of Birth and Death in Child Development — 73
5. The Moment of Death Within the Yearly and Daily Rhythm — 92

Appendix
1. *Preparatory notes for a lecture about death, 1947* — 99
2. *Obituary for Wolfgang Beverley* — 100
3. *Translation of a letter to Tilla Frahm* — 103
4. *An excerpt from Karl König's diary* — 105
5. *Notes for a lecture on suicide, 1963* — 106
6. *Notes from Karl König's last lecture series, 1966* — 111
7. *Karl König's research into the Calendar of the Soul (Richard Steel)* — 115

Notes — 129
Bibliography — 132
Index — 134

Introduction

Michael Bruhn

The gates of birth and death – 'where have we come from before conception?' and 'where are we going after death?' – have always been among the starting points for any form of religious questioning. Eastern religions have given both these questions equal value, focussing on a never-ending cycle of death and rebirth and partly on the question of how this never ending cycle can be escaped or transcended. Western monotheistic religions, notably Judaism and Christianity, as well as Islam, have placed a growing focus on life after death, forgetting the first question or postulating a creation of the human soul out of nothingness at conception or birth. In this way, they have created an increased focus on earthly life, an increased interest in nature and ultimately paved the way for scientific materialism as the predominant belief of our age. If there is only one life on earth, there can be no second chances and everything depends on either our moral performance or our material success in this life. Heaven or hell, eternal bliss or eternal damnation, are in store for us, or there is nothing at all after death and we are nothing but sophisticated machines created by chance and evolution, and neither the existence of life nor the existence of consciousness can be explained.

The 'gate of birth' was also the gate that led Karl König to anthroposophy. On the day he registered for university in Vienna as a medical student he had written in his diary: 'The sea of materialism will rush in upon me, but I shall stand fast. The world and the universe are full of God and full of angels and wonders, full of goodness and anger and full of will.' It was one of his professors, noticing the young student's deeper questions were not answered by conventional science, who gave him the first hint that led him towards discovering anthroposophy as the necessary extension to science that would help him find answers. His lifelong fascination with and interest and research in embryology began here.

Anthroposophy attempts to widen the concept of evolution to include the evolution of human thought, the evolution of consciousness, the evolution of our relationship as human beings to a spiritual world, which lies beyond the reach of our physical sense perceptions, but by no means beyond our experience. In this context, the ancient idea of reincarnation becomes individualised, no longer as an eternal cycle of repetition, but as a means of development for an eternal individual within the greater evolution of human consciousness.

Later, König sometimes spoke of 'embryosophy', indeed a subject full of spiritual beings and wonders, because in the light of reincarnation it deals with the question of how a spiritual human being preparing for a life on earth gets involved in shaping and preparing their future body in its physical development.

Over time, however, the other gate, the 'gate of death' became equally important to Karl König and this is where he takes his starting point for the three lectures on those who have died which form the core of this publication: at any given time, only a small, if growing number of human beings find themselves in an earthly incarnation. The majority are passing through different phases of their development in the spiritual world. They are only separated from us by our inability to perceive them physically and possibly by our non-belief in their existence. In older cultures, the veil between the physical and the spiritual realms of our world was thinner, in our current age he describes it as a thick and very high hedge which has become difficult to penetrate.

Why was this so important for König and his listeners? Such lectures were part of an ongoing programme of further education in anthroposophy for co-workers of the various Camphill communities. These three lectures were held in Newton Dee, a community which had begun to include adults with special needs, some of these may also have been present. The third of the lectures holds a very interesting detail which allows us to understand the kind of cooperation between speaker and audience that König was hoping for and indeed demanded: he mentions a new theme which he says he already tried to introduce a week earlier, but felt unable to bring as 'it was refused'. He does not say in which way or by whom, but in the transcript of the second lecture there is no trace of a first attempt to introduce this particular theme (the development of the three 'higher members' of the human being after death). He must have felt either a lack of openness on the side of his audience or some inhibition of his own thoughts, which made him postpone this theme to a second attempt a week later.

Any speaker who does not just reel off a pre-written script but seeks contact with their audience will know the intense non-verbal communication that takes place and can influence both sides in such a situation. König felt a responsibility to develop anthroposophy as a spiritual base for the curative education and social therapy carried out in the Camphill communities through lectures and other forms of ongoing education. He was also convinced of the need to cooperate with those who had died. Most members of the founding group of Camphill, being largely of Jewish origin, had lost friends or family members in the Nazi extermination camps. Some children with special needs had already died since the opening of the Camphill Schools, as had a number of co-workers or other supporters of the work of Camphill. Every one of these deaths was taken very seriously by König: the anniversaries of their death were remembered, the possible historical significance of each date explored, historical rhythms discovered, astronomical and astrological constellations taken into account, obituaries written. In this book there is an example of these, written by König for Wolfgang Beverly, as well as diary and lecture notes, a letter to the widow of one of his friends, thoughts related to the theme of death in Rudolf Steiner's *Calendar of the Soul,* a related article from a medical journal and one on children's experiences of death and birth.

Long after Karl König's death, when I joined a small Camphill community in Scotland at the age of 25 with little knowledge of anthroposophy, I was struck by the impressive combination of seriousness and light-heartedness with which dying and death were accompanied in these communities. There were no deaths in my immediate surroundings at the time, but there was a telephone information ring linking communities worldwide, and when somebody died elsewhere who was known to the members of my community, I learned that their body remained in their bedroom or was transferred to a chapel of rest and that a wake was held with gospel readings for three days, people taking turns day and night to be present. To accompany this from a distance, we also found a daily time in our own community to meet for a gospel reading. I was very impressed by this positive attitude to death and even more impressed by the conviction that the person who had died would be present and could 'tune in' to the thoughts of the living who were reading for them.

Slowly I learned how anthroposophy describes the path an individual takes after death, which for the first few days consists of a life-panorama (also described by people who have gone through a near-death-experience) and then goes on to describe in great detail the further steps an individual goes through. First they understand their past life on earth and its effects on other people, then they prepare, possibly for some centuries, a future life on earth in very different circumstances. When a friend of mine died in a way that left it unclear whether he might have taken his own life, an experienced Camphill co-worker gave me indications on what I could do inwardly to accompany my friend along his first steps in the spiritual world, how I could keep in contact with him and open myself to the thoughts and ideas he might wish to communicate to me.

All this happened in an open, matter-of-fact way in keeping with one of the important ideas of anthroposophy for the future: that the negation of anything to do with dying and death, so typical for our current western culture, should be overcome and that ever more and more a new kind of imaginative communication across the threshold to the spiritual world should be established, both with the spiritual beings who accompany human life on earth and with the so-called 'dead'. In one of the lectures which are published here, König goes as far as predicting that in future times, communication with those who have died would become a common university subject!

I can see no great likelihood for this to happen in the near future, but König was definitely attempting to teach this particular subject, as derived from anthroposophy, to his fellow co-workers in Camphill. He was also known from time to time to share out particular tasks to individuals or groups in the community, asking them to concern themselves with a particular personality who had died. Sometimes these were historical figures whose ideals and endeavours, he felt, should be better understood and could be helpful for the curative community work in Camphill. But the main attitude in these cases, he insisted, should not be, 'What can they do for us?' but rather 'What can we do for them?' It was obvious to him that a person in the spiritual world would be helped in their development by somebody in earthly life concerning themselves with their ideas and impulses, trying to understand them better and adapting them to their current work on earth. Only with this attitude of selflessness would helpful ideas also stream in the other direction, from the spiritual world into earthly life and work.

To his youth group in Vienna he had given the task to study the lives of those who had died young during the First World War and to try to connect to their unfulfilled aims and intentions. The date of the last meeting of this group, March 11, 1938, as Nazi troops were moving into Vienna, became particularly important for König, both for his 'historic conscience' and constant awareness of the wisdom contained in historic rhythms, and for his personal life. On March 11, 1314, Jacques de Molay, last Grand Master of the Knights Templar had been burned at the stake in Paris. But on his return from the internment camp on the Isle of Man, König discovered that, by a stroke of destiny, their new community home Camphill House was in one of the areas of Scotland where the work of the Templars had been able to continue after 1314. From that time on, March 11 was often mentioned by König – indeed, the Christmas Story he finished and handed over to his wife Tilla on that date bore the dedication 'For March 11, 1947'. This dedication, however, touches a deeper level still, which has, as yet, not found mention anywhere in the biographies of Karl and Tilla König: on March 11, 1942, their fifth child had been still-born.

There are other reasons why thoughts about birth and death, reincarnation, destiny and karma are particularly significant for anthroposophical curative education. The eternal individual, from this point of view, cannot be ill or impaired in any way. But the soul, the life-processes and the physical body can, for whatever reason, be inadequate tools for this individual to come to full expression. In his well-known Christmas Story, written after the death of some children in the care of Camphill, König explored the question what the eternal being of these individuals might be like, now that they had freed themselves from their inadequate tools, and how they might form a community finding a common task for the future. Helping the eternal individual being – shrouded as it may be in difficulties or disabilities, but occasionally shining through – to express itself more and more in this life was always at the centre of König's healing efforts as a doctor and curative educator. We can never know whether the reason for a particular one-sidedness, an illness or disability lies in the past or the future, but the concept of repeated lives on earth, of reincarnation and karma is the single greatest help when working with people whose lives would appear even more meaningless than our own from a materialist point of view. Whatever we meet in life, may have been chosen by ourselves as a necessary challenge when we were preparing this life in the spiritual world. There may be other reasons and we must never use reincarnation as a cheap excuse for inactivity, but the openness and flexibility brought by anthroposophy to curative education and social therapy can be life-changing. It certainly was for me.

Karl König was one of the great pioneers of this forward-looking attitude towards people with special needs. He insisted on the right of every child, however disabled, to attend school and be educated at a time when this idea, now commonplace, was unheard of. With regard to schooling he insisted on age-appropriate content, irrespective of disability. For life and work with adults with disabilities, he insisted on dropping any educational attitude in the adult communities he helped to found and to find appropriate tasks for every individual, so that all could work together on an equal footing. For all these settings he was convinced that no real progress could be made without including and communicating with those who had crossed the threshold into the spiritual world. There are no easy recipes for this, as you will see in the lectures and articles published here, other than an open mind, true imagination and a readiness to change our way of thinking.

During the last months of his life, in his last series of lectures after many years of speaking about karma and reincarnation in a more general way, König returned to the theme of the gates of birth and death. There is a facsimile of his own notes for one of these lectures in the appendix. Based on Steiner's lectures, he calls the gate through which we have come from the past, with everything we have learnt and become, the Gate of the Moon, and the gate towards our future impulses and new abilities, including the ability to experience the ongoing Second Coming of Christ, the Gate of the Sun. Thus Hans Müller-Wiedemann chose 'The Gate of the Sun' as the title of the last chapter in his biography of König.

Karl König passed through this gate into the future on March 27, 1966, and, looking back, it is obvious that he prepared this crossing in rather a conscious way during the previous months. Towards the end of 1965 he had experienced renewed heart trouble. Around Christmas time he noted an experience in his diary, listening to Mahler's *Second Symphony,* 'as if from the second movement on, the experience after death is told to me in all stages.' Probably around the same time he wrote his last, undated poem, full of premonitions of what lay ahead for him, particularly in the following central verses:

> Noises yell into hearkening ears,
> Shrill human speech pierces
> Into the peace-needy heart.
>
> There is the seat of forsaken pain.
> Like a pointing finger it presses
> On the pulse to make it felt,
> Revealing it as existence' source,
> From which our very life wells forth.
>
> Is it an angel's finger?
> Does it herald nearing death?
> Is it a stern indication
> Of an archangel calling you?

The founder of Camphill communities, who had always found inspiration for his work from those who had crossed the threshold before him, moved on to become himself one among their inspiring guides for the future.

I

About Those Who Have Died

Lectures held in Newton Dee,
Scotland, in March 1958

1
The Gate of Birth and the Gate of Death

Sunday, March 16, 1958

Tonight will be a kind of introduction to the next two lectures which lead us to Easter week. In this introduction I feel I have to connect what I have to say in these lectures with something I had to say last Sunday, especially to the young people now working in Thornbury who had asked me to speak to them about the time in which we live.[1] I have the impression that it is not possible today to speak about anything at the moment without connecting to the events and occurrences of our time, although I do not consider that very many people are really aware of what is happening, or what we are facing.[2] Naturally, one is quite unable to face all that is confronting us constantly, but now and then, one should remember the exceptional situation in which we live. Rudolf Steiner pointed to this situation already some years ago. Again and again he tried to draw the attention of those who listened to him to the fateful years which were ahead of them, but there were neither the ears to hear, nor the eyes to see. Therefore, things have developed in a way that probably far surpassed the expectations of Rudolf Steiner himself.

One has the impression that events have moved quicker than were anticipated from the spiritual point of view, and that already things are happening now, which, perhaps, should have happened ten, twenty or thirty years hence. The more we look beyond the barriers of our own narrow existence, the more astonished and overwhelmed we become.

Do not think that I am trying to instil fear into you. Those who are unwilling to see will never see; those who are unwilling to hear will never hear. If I say all these things, I do so only in order to justify them to myself and to no one else, because one has to accept the fact that human nature today is more deaf to the realities than it ever was and it is natural (natural, but not human) that everyone is trying to catch up with themselves, instead of throwing their own lot into this already seemingly lost spiritual battle.

When I tried to make clear to the young friends in Thornbury certain events of our time, I felt compelled to say that our time can be compared with other epochs. Our time, from our particular aspect, is not the very first one. When we look back into the evolution of humankind there were other periods of history, periods of human existence, when humankind was faced with more or less similar situations. For instance, a whole continent was in danger of being destroyed when, in the fourth Atlantean period – at the time when the Turanian people led civilization – certain powers that until then were only known to a small group of initiates were set free, as it were. But instead of these powers being used for good, they were misused. We must imagine that at this time the powers which are enshrined in living seeds of plants were available to human beings, and the Atlantean people (the second, third and then also the fourth periods of Atlantis) had through their initiation the possibility to make use of such seeds, in particular the seeds of the plants which today we call leguminous: beans and peas; they did not look like they do today, but were of the same family. The living powers of these seeds could be

1. THE GATE OF BIRTH AND THE GATE OF DEATH

extracted and used to power flying machines for instance, or other machines which were serving the needs of these people.

These powers came into misuse and from then on a kind of underground destruction worked throughout the whole Atlantean civilization and led in the end to what we know today as the Great Flood and to the destruction of this whole huge continent. If one reads carefully Rudolf Steiner's descriptions of the misuse of these living powers, one finds there is something which, to me, is of great significance. He says that these misused powers were led in such a way that their destructive forces were hindering each other – they were working against each other – and therefore, less harm was done than otherwise would have happened. So, like a double minus gives a plus, this misuse gave a certain amount of possibility, as it were, for the fifth, sixth and seventh Atlantean epochs to continue. Destruction did not set in immediately.

Another period – and we should use our imagination to picture this, because it is necessary for us to see it in this way – was the time which is described in Genesis as the building of the Tower of Babel, when bricks were first introduced for construction. The first bricks were found from about 3000 BC. Before this, people built their houses in quite a different way. Then, suddenly, bricks were used by humankind. With these bricks people wanted to build straight away of course, and again, as it is natural, though not really the human way, they wanted to build as high as possible in order to reach the spirit which had withdrawn from them.

The spirit had withdrawn from them because, only a few years before (and I really mean a few years, not even a century before), the so-called Kali Yuga had started. The start of the Kali Yuga was not the destruction of a continent. Rudolf Steiner describes it in such a way that he said it lasted only a few days, perhaps a few weeks, but during that time human consciousness was dimmed or drowned out; people fell asleep, and only a few were able to wake up again. Those who woke up found themselves in an entirely new condition of existence, because the spiritual world they had been aware of before this inner flood, gradually withdrew. One should try to imagine what it meant that in the year 3101 before Christ, that part of humankind which carried civilization forward, was overcome by this 'flood' that dimmed consciousness of the spiritual world. This affected the countries of the Middle East – Babylonia, Assyria, Persia, Sumeria, the whole of the Levant and Asia Minor (which today is Turkey). And when human beings woke up, the world of the spirit had gone.

At this time the invention of bricks arose, which were used to build physical houses, hearth and home. One can hardly visualize what happened during just these few weeks. If we realize, for instance, that at that time there was a planetary constellation which was only repeated in 1939 when the Second World War started, then we will perhaps understand how our time is intimately connected through the end of the Kali Yuga with what then was the beginning of the Kali Yuga.[3] We should not only know these things, but we should try to experience them; this is so necessary today.

Is it possible that we characterize our time with one idea, as it were, or is it necessary for us to collect details from all sides, in order to describe what mankind is facing today? Thousands of books have been written since the end of the last century, since the end of the Kali Yuga, as if it was the ending of the Kali Yuga that spurred on the mind and soul of people to find out the answer. Most of these books are full of negative statements of what humankind is facing today. Philosophers, scientists and thinkers have tried to evaluate human existence of today in so many

1. THE GATE OF BIRTH AND THE GATE OF DEATH

books and from so many sides. Of course, every one of them sees what is happening in our time from a very specialised point of view. I do not count those who praise our time out of narrow-mindedness, I only speak of those who are really trying to understand what is happening to themselves and their fellow human beings. Nevertheless, I have the impression that one can describe our time in a much shorter, more concise and clearer way by looking at one particular thing. And understanding this one thing we will more or less understand what is happening to us in the various details. I would express it in this way: the value of the human being, the value of things, the value of existence has been lost. This may be easy to say; it is much more difficult to understand, however. If we try to understand this one term: the devaluation – the loss of value – this is the characteristic signature of our time. I think this is the essence of what is really happening at this point of time.

Many people who earnestly try to understand our times have asked themselves how is it possible that in the twentieth century tens of thousands of human beings were killed in a way which is incomprehensible by ordinary human standards? One does not like to think of this again, nor even to be reminded that hundreds of thousands of citizens were shovelled without hesitation into extermination chambers and furnaces. Hundreds of thousands of human lives were sent to death by a simple injection, for the simple reason that they were considered to be valueless because they were either too ill, too old, or too insane to function. Hundreds of thousands of human beings were exterminated simply because they were classified as being of a different 'race'. This was not a battle. This was not war. This was not fighting. It was plain murder. Dear friends, to cast this from our mind and not carry it in our memory; to refuse to try to understand it by turning our back to it, is a crime: the same crime which was committed by those who did the killing.

What is even worse, is that it still goes on – in the east, west, south and north. We know that today in Algeria prisoners are being treated in exactly the same way as the Nazis treated their prisoners. The Russians are doing similar things, and probably all over the world the same is still happening. It can only be understood if we take the words earnestly, that the human being has become valueless – that there is no longer any value attached to human existence. With one idea, one stroke, or one signature, a person`s life can be removed. This was never possible before, because human feelings and emotions were much stronger. Family disputes, clan disputes were fought out, men killed each other, but it was so to speak, an honest fight. Now the dust-heap of a crumbling civilisation has become the grave of millions.

Something similar is happening to all things. For instance, America and all English speaking countries – the whole Anglo-American world is aiming to devalue everything of common use, whether it be chairs, tables, beds, underwear, suits or handkerchiefs. All these things have become valueless. We are even told today that it is more and more necessary not to put any value on these kind of things, but to use and throw them away as quickly as possible, because the greater the demand for consumer goods, the more people find work and employment. So, the more we break, the better we serve society. Thus, our houses are built in such a way that they deteriorate fast; our suits become rags as quickly as possible in order to speed up production. In America, for example, shirts and all underwear can be bought as 'disposables' which are used only once and then thrown away. The value of *things* has been reduced to nought.

It is not only the value of everyday things which is lost. The value of the whole of existence is lost. This can be seen clearly in all that has developed since the beginning of the

1. THE GATE OF BIRTH AND THE GATE OF DEATH

nineteenth century when newspapers began, when every event, every detail was recorded. We now begin to realise the part newspapers as well as radio and television play today. Only gradually am I learning to understand what the song meant that was sung in Vienna when we were young, beginning with the words: 'Am Anfang war die Presse,' (in the beginning was the press or journalism) and afterwards the world was created. Everything that happens today happens without value, because it is depicted, reported and stripped of its real value. What does this mean? What does it mean that we live in a world where the values of the human being, of things and of existence have disappeared?

If you walk with open eyes through an ethnological museum, or through an exhibition showing things used by aboriginal peoples – ignoring pieces of art of bygone periods – but looking at the everyday things which Egyptian or Sumerian people used, or the things which even today are used by some native peoples, who have not yet been invaded by modern civilisation, if you look at their pots and pans, their beds and stools, their weaving and tapestry, you will suddenly become aware that these things are not valueless, but are full of value. They are things which are handed down from father to son and so on. They are imbued with the history of a family, through the impact of each individual. For example, however primitively a hut is built, it means something – it is there to see.

In earlier times human beings were never buried without a great number of everyday things being added to the grave or tomb – a few grains of wheat or rice were put into the dead person's hands, very special garments clothed the body when it was laid into the coffin or grave. For instance, not only were his sword, spear and shield placed around a man to protect his path into the realm of the dead, but sometimes (for a great king, for instance) some of his servants were sacrificed and for them, too, everyday things were added. All this was done because value was placed on the human being, value was placed on things, value was placed on existence.

What does it really mean when we look more deeply into all those things and find they were valued, whereas all that surrounds us today is devalued? I can only use one word to depict what I mean: things today have become *naked*. A naked chair, a naked house, a naked bed, a naked person, a naked kitchen, a naked existence. Is not every one of us stripped of all value, of privacy, of existence, when we face a modern doctor, a psychologist or a psychoanalyst? All who continually try to undress human existence, to find out what kind of feelings, emotions, sensations, are living within this particular person; piercing, and yet not finding anything – gruesomely stripping and tearing all clothes away from the human being. This it is what has happened to our existence. Whatever happens, even if it deviates only a little bit from mass existence, it will be recorded. Suddenly you can read about yourself in the newspaper – where you were last night, where you will go tomorrow; consequently, thousands of people are quite unable to live their own private lives without being photographed or filmed. It is nakedness; everything and everyone is stripped, undressed, in this bare world in which we have to live – this world which is also not clothed any more. The question is, can we clothe it again and what does it mean that the world is naked?

There is only one answer for me. We have lost the spirit; everything and everyone, our whole life, is stripped of the spirit and therefore has become valueless. This is a very grave statement. What does it mean when we say life is spiritless? This is only a general remark of course, and we can do nothing with such a generalisation. Of course we may feel satisfied just to agree that it is lack of spirit. But what is it that has withdrawn? Which parts of spiritual existence have gone so as to leave us entirely naked and bare in our human existence? Again, there seems to be only one possible answer – an answer which shows the truth of the matter – that humankind on earth no longer considers itself to be connected with the other part of humankind, the part which is not on earth.

Today, those who are unborn and those who have died are separated from us. Humankind is divided into two parts, one which is on earth and the other which does not exist any more in their consciousness. These two parts would complete the circle of human existence. And because we do not think, or believe, or count on this much greater part of humanity, everything has become valueless.

In early societies the home is not only used by those who live between birth and death – the home is used by the fathers and forefathers who have died. In Japan, the Shinto religion still places the shrine of the forefathers in the centre of the living family. The grandfathers and grandmothers, the great-great-great-great-grandfathers are all living with the family, eating out of the same plates and pans, sitting round the hearth and leading the man to his work. They guide the children into the world and therefore the whole realm of existence, physical and spiritual, is a united one. It is not so for us any more. We have been driven into this world, as it were, and the gate was closed behind us. And here, at this point, powers of thought have developed. This was necessarily so, otherwise it would have become quite impossible to establish soul-consciousness, but the price we had to pay to develop the emptiness of soul-consciousness is the nakedness of our existence, the valuelessness of the human being, the devalued and naked things around us.

Dear friends, this is exactly what we have to overcome. Step by step a small nucleus of human beings will have to try to re-establish a return, as it were, to the year 3101 before Christ, and form a society (I do not mean a big one) where a spade is again a spade, and work is work, and value is value again. This is not possible by only bringing about beautiful forms, or by shaping things so that they are pleasant to look at, but it is achieved only by creating such forms that help those struggling through life between birth and death to again live consciously with those who have died. We have to develop more and more images and ideas in such a way that the dead can participate. In answer to the question, 'What is the language which those who have died understand?' Rudolf Steiner once said very clearly that the language of anthroposophy is the only one which the dead understand.[4]

Rudolf Steiner also warned: 'The dead do not speak in English, they do not speak in German, nor in Russian; they speak in such a way that only heart and soul can understand them.'[5] We have not only to learn to speak the language of the dead, we have also to learn to develop images which we can share with the dead, because only then will this wall of thoughts, which more or less separates the world of the dead from the world of the living, be penetrated. When we have died and we look back on this earth as a globe – or also if we are not yet born and come down and circle around the earth – it shows a very special appearance; in such a way that the eastern half of the globe (Asia for instance) appears blue and lilac, whereas the western part appears red and orange. So that all the parts of America and the Atlantic Ocean, right down to the western parts of Europe, appear in red and orange.

In between there is a light green which goes along Europe including Greece. For those who have died there appears to be something like a golden crystal in the Holy Land. To share such an image is important; for instance of how the eastern part of the earthly globe shines, as it were, with its darkness through the glow of light around it – and thereby it appears to be blue. Whereas the western part radiates its inner light through a darker cover and thereby appears yellowish, orange or red. And in between is the mediating colour of green.[6] To carry such an image up and offer it to the dead in order to share it with them without any intellectual explanation is of utmost importance. Or, for instance, to know that when those who have died have laid aside their physical body, the ether body rises up and out of the ether body all the memories and experiences of the past life rise also. After this they do not acually 'lay aside' the astral body but they widen it and it exhales throughout the whole cosmos. This is an image – a true picture of reality. At the same time, in order to keep up the conciousness of the 'I' and the soul after death, the angel enters much more intimately into the 'I', the angel permeates the 'I' and the soul and by these means every human being after death develops a certain amount of consciousness of the events of the spiritual world, even if it is a kind of dream consciousness. With this angel other angels are then united, and in order to heighten our consciousness, archangels then also permeate our existence and we 'wake up', as it were.

Under this pressure we develop quite new organs which lead us on during our life between death and rebirth. In this way they lead us into what Rudolf Steiner described as spirit-man, life-spirit and spirit-self. If we imagine this and try to learn and understand what Rudolf Steiner wanted to give to us, then we will gradually understand that out of the seed of earth existence, out of the foliage of the enfolding memories, there grows the flower of spirit-man, unfolding the petals, and within this, the other two organs – the life-spirit and spirit-self. And in this unfolding flower the possibilities of imagination, inspiration and intuition develop.

These are the forces that guide us through the world between death and rebirth. In intuition the spirit-self leads us back more and more into our new existence. We have to learn that once upon a time – and in some societies untouched by 'civilisation' still today – beyond the abyss of the Kali Yuga, as it were, human beings could still look to all those who had died and thereby experience all this. We have to look in a different way in order to bring value into our existence. We have to look to all those who are going to be born – not to their bodies only, but we must know that they come from the spirit and will need to take their place in this world, and that we have to receive them. This is the only way in which things will become clothed again and so regain their value.

There is a lecture which Rudolf Steiner gave in 1916 in which he says that the events of our time are going in such a direction that not far from the year 2000, orders will come from America, from the west, to extinguish the possibility of individual thought; whereas in the east – and I think he means Russia – he says something will develop which one can only describe as the irreverence for the unborn child.[7] I think it is worth trying to imagine that at the same time as one thing will come from the west and the other will come from the east, what Rudolf Steiner expected to happen around the year 2000 will probably happen much sooner through the events of the last twenty years. If we can imagine these two dangers for our times we will understand why it is so necessary for us today – at least for a few of us – to become aware of what it means to remain, or perhaps to become once more a human being.

I do not think I should add anything more at this moment, but during this period of Lent we could all benefit positively if we direct our thoughts to all of humankind and consider that birth and death are only portals. We must recognise that the greater part of humankind exists beyond these portals and that we are one with them. We must unite with them in order to bring about what is so necessary to do.

2
Bridges to Those who Have Died

Sunday, March 23, 1958

Last Sunday we looked at what lies behind many of the events taking place today. We discovered that these symptoms could be described simply by saying that values have been lost: the value of things, of existence and of the human has been reduced to nought. When we looked further into what it means that these values have been lost, we discovered that it means nakedness and bareness. Everything has become naked – it has become devalued – it lies, as it were, in front of everybody and everything without any form of protection, and therefore has become valueless. When we sought the reason for this, we came to the conclusion that it is because humankind has forgotten that living on earth is only part of a greater whole. There is a vast army of those who live between death and rebirth, and because we are cut off from the other or better part of our existence, we are driven into nakedness, into a state of being without any value. One of the foremost tasks of our time to build a bridge again that can lead us back into this land where we can meet and unite with those who have died, in order that they may provide the protecting clothes and sheathes for us and for everything that exists here on earth. Very many things which happen today will be understood only if we learn to take this knowledge to heart.

Not very long ago – I think it is only a few months – a book was published describing very interesting research carried out during 1955 and 1956 on Easter Island. It was not an unknown person who wrote this book, but the famous Thor Heyerdahl, leader of the famous Kon-Tiki Expedition some years ago.[1] A book like this is fascinating because of what it adds to general knowledge of humankind. And yet one is horrified by the way misunderstanding, intellectual pride and inability to make contact with the spirit, rules over those well-meaning, good-hearted Europeans who conducted such an expedition. Why? Because for them, of course, the world of which I spoke, the greater part of humankind beyond the threshold of this life, is non-existent.

I would like to go into some detail, because it will explain what we are trying to understand. The island is called Easter Island because it was discovered on an Easter Sunday, by a Dutch voyage which landed there inadvertently in the year 1722. Since that day this very strange island has been of special interest to those who investigate the history and development of humankind, because certain things are found there which do not exist anywhere else in the world.

In the British Museum in London there is a huge figure in basalt, about six metres (20 ft) high. It is one of several hundreds of such figures which can be found on Easter Island. Incomprehensibly shaped, with very strange features, very strangely shaped heads, they stand on the cliffs around the shores of this island. They do not face the Pacific Ocean, but look down on to the island. No one knows how they were sculptured and no one can understand at all how such figures could be transported several miles and lifted up without any machinery. Furthermore, every one of these figures carries a helmet, about as heavy as the weight of two elephants, balancing on its head.

2. BRIDGES TO THOSE WHO HAVE DIED

Engraving of a European explorer on Easter Island.

After that Dutch ship, several other ships also visited Easter Island, with the consequence that more and more of the original population died out, until at the beginning of the twentieth century not more than a hundred true native inhabitants were left, but now about a thousand live there. Most of the figures have fallen down. In spite of the many expeditions, no solution has been found to the riddle of these figures.

Heyerdahl, the first European to do so, found something else. The natives are still able to remember what their fathers thought, what their grandfathers did and what their great-grandfathers experienced. The stream of family memory is still running through their veins and their consciousness is an entirely different one from ours today. On this island – and some of the previous explorers already discovered this – there are many caves, all of which are absolutely empty. So far, no-one has found anything in them except a few animal and human bones. But one night, when Heyerdahl was nearly asleep, there was a scratching at the wall of his tent, and when he went out one of the natives stood there with a bag in his hand and said to Heyerdahl: 'My wife sends you these' and he handed over some figures made of stone which Heyerdahl had never seen before. They were very strange forms, beautifully carved, of bearded men, elephants, whales; strange animal and human forms, some large and some small. When Heyerdahl asked the native where he had got them, the man gave no answer.

It took Heyerdahl weeks of cunning, research, persuasion and lying before it was possible for him to get a first hint what these were, but it was he, as the first European, who found out that each family on Easter Island (at least the more important families, who for the most part now inhabit the island) possesses one, two or even three caves, about which no-one except the family know. Only one member of the family, usually the father, knows the entrances to these caves and before the father dies he passes the secret to the eldest son or eldest daughter. These caves are the most important treasures which the family possesses. For centuries these figures had lain in them, a few of which had come into Heyerdahl's possession. The forefathers, many generations past, had made these figures.

Now imagine what follows. All the natives had become Christians. For the last twenty or thirty years a most wonderful old Roman Catholic priest had lived on this island and although he had spent his whole life trying to understand the island, not a single one of his flock ever told him anything about these caves. He did not believe Heyerdahl at first when he told him about them, because the natives lead two lives, so to speak: an outer life – a Christian, everyday life – and one that remained hidden in the depths of their soul. In the realm of the depths they lived with their forefathers and with the dead. It was out of this realm that they had built the huge stone figures in the image of those who had died. These caves are nothing but the real symbols, the realities and backbone of the moral existence out of which they live.

When Heyerdahl asked the two or three who had revealed this secret to him why it was they had told it to him and no-one else, the reply was, 'Because you are one of us! There is an old saga which tells that one day a white one will come who is none other than our former chief, and that one is you.' Of course, Heyerdahl mocks about it in his book, saying how happy and lucky he was that this was possible, but he did not consider that perhaps it was true. He did not consider that perhaps he would never have found Easter Island, nor would he have found the current in the Pacific Ocean which carried him away from South America to Polynesia on a raft, if he had not once upon a time been one of these who still inhabit Easter Island.

We should earnestly consider such things. We should learn to see the relationship with those who have died in a new light, otherwise no understanding will come about, neither of ordinary nor extraordinary events which face us time and again. What is so necessary for today, is to ask ourselves how can we build a bridge into the land of the dead – what is the substance of this bridge – how can we possibly construct it? There is only one answer. We have no other bridge, no means to reach into the land where they live, other than our power of thought. It lies in our thinking. Only when we begin to take this earnestly and not only know it, but write it down and so drive it home, does it become alive within us. If, day after day, we learn to say to ourselves that it is in thinking, in our power of thought, that we are able to build the bridge across the River Lethe, the classical river of forgetfulness, and walk in our thoughts over it. Only then will we really begin what is so important for our time.

Our thoughts, our ordinary thoughts, can only be expressed at any given moment when they are clothed in language. We must learn to transform language in order to reach those who are dead. If we think that our ordinary language will be understood by those beyond the threshold, we are wrong, because our language is a national thing. We speak either German, English, French or whatever other language there may be, but those who have died are neither French nor German, nor are they American or Russian, they are only human. We should realise that there is no nation beyond the threshold, that we cannot reach those who have died with English, German or Russian words. We should make it our conviction which pulsates through our entire being, that in this part of humankind, the part beyond the threshold, there are no Norwegians, no Dutch, no Italians no Spaniards; there are only human beings. In our national language we are quite unable to reach them. In our ordinary speech we are quite unable to make ourselves understood and, what is worse, to make them understand what is happening here on earth. Only if we begin to de-nationalise our language, to dematerialise our words, and to bring about that the Word again becomes a seed from which a sprouting plant reveals the spiritual content, then will we start to prepare the ground for a new connection with those who have died. When the dead look at the field of language of today, when they look at the way in which we think, how our thoughts are rushing about aimlessly, colourlessly, it appears from above as if our field of language was a stony desert, barren, where nothing grows. Every attempt, to re-enliven a word, to bring a seed to the point of sprouting so that at last the plant can begin to grow, will make it possible for the dead to come and pluck such a flower, receiving out of it a message from this earthly ground.

This is an image which we should try to understand more and more. This is an image which directs us towards Easter, because in it appears the light of the Risen One, who can then walk through the garden which human beings have tried to prepare in the land of thought and language. When Rudolf Steiner speaks about the language of the dead, he refers to our earthly language as being a kind of carpet which hides the land beyond the threshold from us living here on earth, and that only when we have died do we start to unfold, to dissolve each word. When we do the same here on earth, we are, as it were, in unison with those who have died; we work together with them, we reach up towards them. We do not speak in simple terms with them, but try to go into the different hidden layers of language, and reveal the meaning for them. For instance, we can make clear how cosmic thoughts have built up our words, and how we can dissolve those words in trying to realise cosmic thoughts. We can try to realise, for example, that a word like 'left' or 'right' is not simply left and right, but that 'left' is a thing which is also sinister, dark and clumsy, and that 'right' is really a thing which is right and bright, light and righteous.

If this begins to live and work in us, our communication with the dead will become possible. The dead do not understand any abstract words; words like 'love' or 'joy' or 'decision' are quite impossible for them. If we want to re-enliven language, if we want to re-enliven thinking, it is necessary to speak with them continually in the form of verbs, because living activity, feeling, is still contained in the verbs. In this way language reaches upwards.

This change in our way of thought, the necessity to reshape and reform our way of thinking is so urgent. We have to learn, for example, to have entirely new ideas, because in the land where the dead live, things are entirely different. If we go on in our narrow way of thinking we shall never unfold and rejuvenate our thoughts to such an extent that the garden of which I spoke can really be established. We have the means to rejuvenate our way of thinking through anthroposophy. This is not something that we can merely learn, but is something that we have to continually practise. For example, we can try to picture an aspect of reincarnation. We know from Rudolf Steiner that reincarnation works in such a way that out of the body of this present life the head of the next life will be formed. In addition to the head, a new body is formed which more or less comes out of the stream of heredity.

Again, this body is transformed into the head of the coming life and a new body is added to it. But such knowledge must not remain merely abstract knowledge that we can just write down as, 'Our head is the result of the body of our last incarnation.' Nothing will come of it in this way; you can repeat it a hundred times and it will still mean nothing. Unless you begin to struggle

2. BRIDGES TO THOSE WHO HAVE DIED

to understand and find out how our hands and fingers, our arms and chest, our abdomen, our legs and feet are transformed into our head organisation, nothing will come of this knowledge. We need to practise in our imagination how the long bones of the limbs turn into the round ones of the skull, and we need to try time and again to understand that the limbs are free and mobile, whereas in the head they are grown together, packed together, without the possibility of moving; everything in the head is enclosed, fully formed, hardened and ossified. But in the limbs everything is free, is mobile and goes from the centre into the periphery.

Such images cannot be thought about or imagined often enough, because then we carry something upwards which becomes alive when we learn to understand that a limb reaches out further and further into the distance, the head is the result. It is, as it were, the fruit of the tree of the body, and although this tree reaches back through time and space into the distant past, the fruit nevertheless belongs to it. The head is the fruit which ripens on the tree of the body, though the tree grows in one life and the fruit ripens in the next one. Out of this fruit a new tree begins to grow, and out of this tree again another fruit – a fruit that I bear myself as it is the 'I' that goes through incarnations, creating its own body. The shaping of my head reaches back, and I learn to understand more and more of what is past. My limbs reach out into the future and I learn to understand what it means to become – that with each deed that I perform, I prepare the fruit of the head for my next incarnation.

It is worthwhile to imagine what it means if a few people are thinking like this about forms being created that transcend the usual limits of time and space. These are thoughts that those who have died can understand. From this they can learn to understand what they have failed to understand while they were alive here on earth. We can go on reshaping our thinking in order to help the dead, and then we may understand, for instance, that the fruit of the head, though it is the fruit of the tree of my body, would not be able to ripen and would not be able to form itself, if the whole cosmos did not work on it during life between death and rebirth, forming it, as it were, in its own image. So that from all directions of the heavens, from everywhere, the cosmos with its beings is working on the head organisation of those soul-spirit beings who are to be born. And – excuse me for saying it in this way – we can imagine how millions and billions of human heads are continually being formed in the cosmos of our planetary system, how thousands of beings, together with millions of 'I's, are continually working, forming, preparing the fruits.

We can also learn that something quite different happens when our chest organisation is formed. This is built by only half the cosmos, the part which is the east of the cosmos: not the east which we call the east (although this has something to do with it), but the part of the cosmos which belongs spiritually to the sun and to the process of becoming. It is similar to the eastern half of the earth which appears in a blue colour to those who have died.

We can also learn how out of the depth of the earth our limbs are formed, and how the three – head, chest and limbs – are united to create the human form here on the surface of the earth between the heights of the cosmos and the depths of the earth.

You see, if we look towards the gate of birth and have such thoughts and make living ideas out of them, we open a pathway to those who have died that helps them find their way towards a new life on earth, to be born again into earthly reality. But if we look towards death, we can learn that the moment of death is an entirely different event for the one who has just died from what is normally imagined by those living on earth.

If we look back to our birth we look into the dark – we have no memory of the event, we only know that once upon a time we must have been born, otherwise we would not be here; but to remember how it happened is given to hardly any one of us. It is quite different for those who have died, because the moment of death is the most vivid, the most glorious recollection. This moment is never forgotten throughout the whole afterlife. It is the central moment to which we continually look back in order to know how to direct our existence. After death, for a few days while we still possess an etheric body, we experience within this ether body the whole planetary constellation of our moment of death: this planetary constellation surrounds us like a huge amnion. Then we leave this and enter with our spirit into the 'east', into the sun realm. We may sometimes hear, for instance when a Freemason dies, that they have 'entered the eternal east'. This is because somewhere they still have a knowledge that those who die enter the sphere of the sun, the sphere of the cosmic east.

We have to try to acquire such ideas and such images again, not only to enliven our thinking for our own sake, but to begin to prepare the ground which is so necessary and important for those who have died. For those who have died the 'I' is the only thing they possess. It is no longer a pliable 'I' like ours here on earth, because here we acquire ideas, we change and move, but as soon as we are dead we feel our 'I' with all its experiences, more or less like we feel the outer world here on earth. We also have to realise that here on earth we look out from within, but yonder, we look from all around to the within. We need to practise this here, to be able to help those who have died.

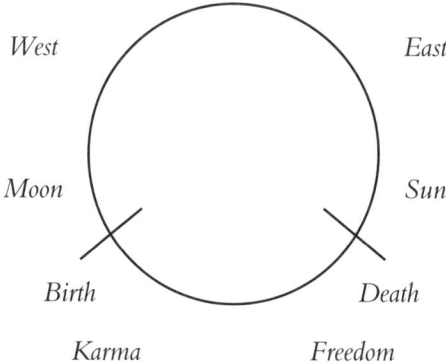

The gate of birth in the west and the gate of death in the east.

If we allow the gate of birth and the gate of death to become objects of deepest meditation for us, we begin to realise that the doors of birth and death are shown to us in daily life in an image: the moon and the sun moving around us are the gates of birth and death. All who are born enter only through the sphere of the moon, and all those who die go out only through the sphere of the sun. The past – karma, the laws of necessity – are all connected with the sphere of the moon, but the future and the element of freedom – the process of becoming and developing – these are all connected with the gate of death, with the sun. If we enliven our gaze and see the moon as the gate of birth, and if we look at the sun as the gate of death, and if these two, the past and the future, become alive in us, then we shall begin to recognise what is sun and what is moon in every human being we meet. We can also ask ourselves what is karma and what is freedom in my connection to everyone. If we do not merely speculate about it, but try to experience it, to imagine it, then bonds are established once more that will weave a new possibility, out of which the bridge will be built into the kingdom of the dead.

Let me finish with another image. Rudolf Steiner once

2. BRIDGES TO THOSE WHO HAVE DIED

told us that in our time it is necessary to realise that the feeding of the five thousand was a miracle which Christ performed in order to make human life possible in the fifth Post-Atlantean epoch.[2] When we read the story of the multiplication of bread in the gospel, we may be struck by the fact that the location is first called a desolate or deserted place – one might even say a desert – and in the next sentence Christ bids the five thousand to sit down on the green grass. This is the garden of our thinking where the flowers will grow if only we nourish our thinking so that it turns from a place of desolation to one full of green grass.

Dear friends, those who have died are more real than we ever think, and the meadow which people can create is the meadow where the dead can walk. If this is done, the sun of the Risen One will shine, enabling all the flowers to grow which are needed so much. It is this which builds the bridge from those on earth to those on the other side.

3
The Path Beyond Death

Palm Sunday, March 30, 1958

Last time we looked at certain thoughts and special images in order to acquaint ourselves with the regions where the greater part of humankind is continually assembled, living and working to prepare their next life on earth. We will have experienced how difficult it is to approach the sphere where we all have to live each time between death and rebirth. We saw how ordinary thoughts cannot penetrate into the land of the dead, how this land is guarded, how it is surrounded by a huge hedge. Everyday thoughts are refused entry, everyday ideas are rejected, and everyday emotions are not wanted at all. With self-knowledge we will time and again experience certain misgivings which arise because we do not like to be rejected. So again and again we will find ourselves abandoning our approach to the sphere of the dead. We will not only find ourselves abandoning our efforts to enter this sphere, but we will find a veil of forgetfulness shrouds our consciousness. We might live for weeks or months on end without a single thought about the huge army of those who have died that is around us; they continually lead us, continually try to approach us, continually want to permeate our existence and take part in what we experience.

    We should take this to heart and remember it, for time and again we have to make these efforts against the odds

3. THE PATH BEYOND DEATH

that our present age continually sets up by endeavouring to cloud, to hide, to cut off the so-called dead from those who are living here on earth. That is why last time I brought some of the ideas of Rudolf Steiner as exercises of imagination with which we can train the one tool which is given to us here on earth – the power of thought – in order to reach up to the world of the dead.

We came to the image of the desert of our everyday thoughts and discovered that only when we try to mould these thoughts in such a way that their meaning, their spiritual idea, is released, then will this stony desert be transformed into a garden where those who have died can walk and pick the flowers. In a lecture Rudolf Steiner described how the dead come for nourishment to those who are asleep.[1] The dead come to those who were their friends and relatives looking for and wanting to take up real ideas, wonderful and beautiful imaginations, because this is their food. We should not question what we human beings can mean to the dead, or what we humble people can give them. This would utterly misjudge and misunderstand our possibilities. In the same way as we are able to help them, they are willing to help us, but we have to prepare ourselves for this to happen. It is one of the duties of being human. In later centuries, no doubt, there will be universities where people can be taught to perform these duties and no human being will be able to work on earth in a proper way if he is unwilling to unite and connect himself with the so-called dead.

Steiner's lecture to which I just referred was given in October 1913 in Bergen, Norway. I mention this for the special reason that a few days before he gave this lecture, Steiner had revealed for the first time in the course of five lectures what he called *The Fifth Gospel*. From then on, week after week until the beginning of the First World War, he not only lectured and continued to lecture on chapters of the Fifth Gospel, but also revealed more and more openly the land of which we are trying to speak. The two go together, and this needs to be recognised. We will come back to this at the end of our deliberations, but I want to point this out.

If we follow up Rudolf Steiner's revelations we usually find that it is not only one thing that he reveals, there are usually two together which are intimately connected. For example, during the years 1908 to 1912 he revealed the Second Coming of Christ and at the same time he gave all the lecture cycles and many single lectures about the various gospels: this was not one, but two subjects. On the one hand, Christ in the twentieth century and on the other hand the revelation of the Mystery of Golgotha in the four gospels. Then in 1913 he went one step further, and spoke about a fifth gospel and with it the world around the Second Coming of Christ, which is the world of the dead. These revelations culminated in the six lectures he gave at Easter 1914 in Vienna about which we will say a few words later.[2] In a similar way, as if it were out of a renewed Christianity, the knowledge of karma and reincarnation was born. The land of the dead, life between death and rebirth, was unfolded out of a new revelation of the Fifth Gospel, out of a new revelation of the true events which surround the being of the Christ, and this to an extent that had never happened before in any of the mysteries. Here it was revealed for humanity, whether prepared or not. We should understand this with the greatest possible earnestness.

I would also like to mention something very special about life after death. In the same way as human beings here on earth, in life between birth and death, consist of four levels of being: physical, etheric and astral bodies and the 'I', so, when we are beyond the threshold after the moment of death, we also unfold our existence in a fourfold way.

3. THE PATH BEYOND DEATH

There we also possess four levels of being and in the same way as our four bodies gradually establish themselves here on earth when we grow from childhood to youth, in the same way, after death, all four 'bodily' levels unfold step by step. We gradually become aware of those bodies. After we have crossed through the gate of death our 'I' almost corresponds to what in this life we call our physical body.

As well as the etheric body and astral body, Rudolf Steiner described three higher parts of the human being, as yet fairly undeveloped. The spirit-self is the part of our astral body that we have transformed and refined through our own efforts. The life-spirit is the transformed and refined etheric body. Finally, and least developed of all, spirit-man is our transformed physical body.

Rudolf Steiner describes the 'I' here on earth as having a more or less fluid existence. I do not mean liquid, but a fluid state – flowing, changing its form of existence. Day after day our 'I' is renewed. We know it is the same 'I', but it has new experiences, it reacts in a varied way; more and more new impressions come to our 'I' and they come as it passes through the portals of waking and sleeping. But behind the gate of death the 'I' becomes fixed: it has been formed, it is there, and it is, as it were, unchangeable, unalterable. Rudolf Steiner described the 'I' after death as a fully formed spiritual gestalt resulting out of the past life and formed through death itself, and nothing can be changed in this 'I'. He describes it more fully by saying that if we were to look over a field, all the different growing plants would be visible to us; in such a manner we see our 'I' after death. At that moment we would say to ourselves, 'What do we see?' At that moment we see our 'I' as the great panorama of our existence on earth. All that we have thought, all that we have experienced, is now laid out before us through the unfolding ether body. Our existence, in the form of our experiences, is before us. Rudolf Steiner calls this the 'I'.

This is the first level of our existence after death. Here on earth we experience things continually and every day anew; at the moment of death our experiences cease and all that we have experienced, all that our life was here on earth, is unfolded like a great script, or tableau – and we look at this in the same way as here on earth we look into the world around us. Imagine looking at ourselves. Our self is now outside and we behold it. There is our childhood, with father, mother and certain events which stand out; teachers and relatives; perhaps an outing which is especially vivid in our memory; then the first years of our youth, the years of work, our children, our experiences in later life: All this is I; but the 'I' in this situation has become the world, the only world we can perceive: there is nothing else around me but 'I' myself. This is my 'I' and I breathe in the spirit-language of it, and look upon this panorama and know it is 'I'. When this phase is over, there is a new experience.

The second level of our existence appears, or we might say, we become aware of it. We feel our gaze – although one can no longer speak of eyes – drawn to one splendid point of our life, and then it is suddenly turned and drawn to another part of our life. It is as if we were to stand at a window and somebody came from behind, took our head and turned it to look at one tree, then lifted it to look at a cloud, and then turned it to look at a meadow. As soon as we give ourselves up to this, we know that it is our spirit-self that begins to surround us. Within this spirit-self spiritual being-hood appears around us. It might have been an angel who turned our gaze, or it might have been one of the Archai who pointed to an other event. Around us, so to speak, in the sphere of the spirit-self, which becomes more and more apparent, being-hood is awakening and our loneliness comes to an end. Other spiritual beings appear around us.

When this phase of existence is more fully worked through, another new experience comes and we feel our existence permeated by powers of life. Sprouting, springing powers of life weave through our being and we feel renewed and revived, but we have to learn something about these powers of life forces. We learn to experience that whatever living being we now touch with these powers of life in our surrounding, now dies. They die in such a way that soul and spirit forces are freed out of them, but life itself disappears, withers away. This is an entirely new experience because only at this point can we learn to understand what the spirit of life is in reality: the life-spirit is unfolded around us.

After this a fourth experience comes about. At this point the spirit-man is born. Rudolf Steiner says that it is more and more difficult to find the right words to describe what is to be experienced here. He tries to explain that the powers of spirit-man are now such that they destroy all form, all gestalt.

These are the four stages of our existence between death and rebirth. If you try to relate such knowledge to those who have already died, or if, for instance, you try to find the right images in order to help those who died without any understanding of spiritual science, then this can help them relate to what they now experience. We can try to guide them so that they can find their own 'I', then to their spirit-self, their life-spirit, their spirit-man. And if you are able to connect yourself intimately with all that Rudolf Steiner has so beautifully described, you will be able to see that this formed-out 'I' – what has been described as our tableau after death – may appear to you, for instance, in the form of the youth in Goethe's fairy tale. The spirit-self, directing the gaze to the various points of the 'I' is the Old Man with the Lamp; the life-spirit which, when touching anything makes it die, is the Beautiful Lily; and the spirit-man, which is the highest level of being in us, and which, beyond the threshold destroys form, is like the Green Snake which, after it has sacrificed itself and built the bridge, falls in thousands of precious stones into the river.

If we offer such images to those who have died – like the youth, for instance, lying dead surrounded by the magic circle of the snake, and the bird hovering above directing the rays of the sun to his body, and the beautiful lily and all the other figures around it – this is true nourishment. Those who have died can take this in, and it will change within their souls into spirit-knowledge with which they will understand their own existence. In this way we shall start to serve those who need us or ask for our help.

Last time I described the difference in experience between the moment of birth and the moment of death. Birth is veiled in darkness. We don't know anything about the moment of our birth. The moment of death is entirely different, because it is the high point, it is the light that shines continually, without interruption, through the life between death and rebirth. It is continually before us. It radiates and is a focal point of consciousness. The further we go away from it, the stronger it radiates towards us. Further back, beyond this point was our physical body which we have laid down.

After death, many people are able to follow what happens to their body which they have left behind. Whether it is handed over to the powers of decay by being buried, or to the powers of fire when it is burned, makes no difference. They observe this objectively and in a detached way, like we observe the weather. In a similar way they look down on their body and accept as a complete necessity that it disintegrates: they let it go with no concern, so to speak. However, it is different with the ether body.

I will describe it now not with regard to its *content,* because its content represents us, it represents our own 'I' –

3. THE PATH BEYOND DEATH

the person we were in the past between birth and death. We will now look away from the person to the ether body itself. Not many who have died are able to see this immediately and clearly and know what it means, because in the same way as here on earth we have to learn to understand earthly existence, they also have to learn to understand life after death. If we imagine this – which we can do with the help of anthroposophy – then we will understand that within this ether body there are two different kinds of forces. One force will disappear, will leave us: it is the life body or life force of all living creatures; it will deteriorate and die. (In a similar way the life forces of the whole earth will disintegrate.) However, there are other powers which will appear within this ether body. Rudolf Steiner describes how the second force is like the growing forces, powers of life of young shooting plants, and that these powers of life radiate and begin to permeate the ever-expanding ether body, like tiny little flames.[3] They are the powers of the Christ-impulse which began at the moment when the blood of Christ on the cross flowed into the earth.

Furthermore, Steiner describes how in the ever-widening expansion of our ether body after death there appears, stretched out, the essential substance of the body of Christ. Thus we can imagine an ever-widening ether body, wide as the whole firmament, and in it the living powers of the Christ, springing out of the blood which had permeated the earth. And imprinted there, in this shroud of our ether body, the body of the Christ himself can be found. This is the true image of the Holy Shroud. If we can follow this, then we can understand that the body laid in the coffin is the altar; behind this altar the ether shroud of our own ether body widens, and within this ether shroud the body and the life of the Christ appears – the bread and the wine. Immediately after death a service is celebrated, from which those who have died learn the certainty that the human being does not perish, but goes on to live as spiritual content of the earth.

This, dear friends, can be our Easter message this year: in spite of everything that happens, human beings do not perish but live on as the spiritual content of this earth. In spite of everything that we have to meet today, this conviction, this certainty, this determination, this absolute 'yes' to the future of humankind, this we should inscribe into our hearts in the name of Christ.

The lecture from which I have quoted was the last one that Steiner gave in the various series of lectures on the Fifth Gospel. One has the impression that the whole of the Fifth Gospel was given in order to bring the message that, as a spiritual entity, the human being will not perish. A few weeks after this Rudolf Steiner went to Vienna, where he gave the lecture cycle *The Inner Nature of Man and our Life between Death and Rebirth*. If you care to study this lecture cycle, individually or in groups, you will find that Rudolf Steiner closes each one of the six lectures with a special sentence.[4] The first two lectures he closes with the words EX DEO NASCIMUR, the third and fourth with the words IN CHRISTO MORIMUR, and the last two with the words PER SPIRITUM SANCTUM REVIVISCIMUS. With these sentences he inscribed into his revelations – into the sphere of the dead – the endeavour of Christ for our time. It is as if Steiner inserted the Christ of the twentieth century into this new revelation of all that Steiner had experienced with the dead as the life between death and rebirth and in this way he could reveal the Fifth Gospel.

Today, dear friends, is not only Palm Sunday, but also the anniversary of Rudolf Steiner's death. It is the thirty-third year after he passed into the spirit realm and left his body which he wore during his life. It is due to him that human beings can meet in the way we have met tonight, and that one is able to hear such a message – even 33 years after his death.

I will speak now entirely out of a personal experience, and I hope you will forgive me for doing this. When those of you who are older look back to the time when Rudolf Steiner died, and try to remember what the day of March 30 meant to you during the past years, then we can see that a great change has taken place since then. To begin with this day was overwhelmed with grief and pain through the intimate connection of the heart with the one who had died. It was clearly an outstanding day in the year. It was difficult to meet other people on this day because the pain, the grief and the sorrow were so great. As always, time heals wounds, so the grief has gradually died away, and this immediate and intimate connection with the one who had left this earth receded more and more. Gradually a kind of division came about which became more and more marked in the last few years. On the one side was the historic personality, Rudolf Steiner, and on the other the essential being that was within this personality. With a certain amount of distance we can gradually see the standing of the historic personality at the end of the nineteenth and beginning of the twentieth century, we can begin to discern his place in history and recognise the human being with all its karma, with the friends around him, with his pupils, and the failures of those surrounding him. To this also belongs the Anthroposophical Society which still tries to preserve the historic person. On the other hand there rises in ever greater light what the legacy is, what the sacrifice was, what the being within this personality has been and is. I have the impression that we will gradually see this more and more. As the man fades into the distance of history we will see the essential being rise ever clearer, lighter, into the future. If we follow this being, we will prepare his entry into this earthly realm again.

This we should observe with as much objectivity as we can develop within ourselves – not judge, but know. Know what he gave, what he created and what was in him. To this our spirit should look, because it is a rising spirit-star which leads into the future and it bears the message which I have tried to convey to you. One can almost feel, almost see, the Risen Christ speaking this message.

Let us take this with us because by so doing those who have died will be with us. They will know that not only has Christ risen as the light within their midst, but also that humankind on earth is not lost.

II

Poems

The Death of Adalbert Stifter

As you put the knife's edge
To your throat
The sharp steel touched
The warm skin;
As the power of indignity
Directed your hand
And you wounded

The infinite stream of blood.
In this moment
That severed both your life and death,
It was clarity of spirit,
Not confusion
Surrounding your inner being.
Narrow paths of perception had widened,
Now the hand that once
Had led you through life's phases
Directed you to the portal.
That was the way for your stride now,
Not back, no, back no more.

You stood before your self,
Saw the tapestry of your life;
Distress, humiliation,
The incessant pains
That held you in their clutch
From early every morning,

Never to release you
Throughout the day.
And when the evening came,
Night fell around you.
Then it was the fear
That gripped your heart
And ill and weary,
Helpless, hopeless
Was your entry into the dark,
Into the realm of night.
No use were prayer and folded hands,
For never had your faith
Enough light and strength to give.
You felt that pious habits
Were mere deceit and false,
A foredoomed quest
To save oneself from sin
And hold off all misery.

You saw all those
Who stood by you,
Given to guide and aid,
Yet their help was hindrance
Their love obstruction
And their affinity the fetter
Which rendered hopeless
Your attempted refuge
From the dungeon of yourself.

Oh, how powerless and tormented!
Imprisoned in a body
That conveyed but pain
And animal drive,
Plantlike numbness
And instinct's lust.

To this came also knowing
That every human bond
With it severance brings;
That every word of goodness
Hate and envy breed,
That each warm touch of hand
Heartless cold will find
In this earthly world.

Thus, for distress and weakness
Torment and pain,
You could not find the strength –
Could not redeem.
For you were damned
And forsaken!
Someone who, so it seemed
God had no care for,
Had cast out and abandoned
In the cold inflicted land
That is this world.

And all the many people
Seemed in league with God
And so, opposed to you!
Every other person
Had faith and love and hope;
From altars high could they all
The sacraments receive
And sustain them deep within.

They could have peace of heart
And their souls could
Unite with the sun,
Befriend the sky and clouds,
The light and dawning day,

The colour flush and song of larks,
The wandering stars
And mellow moon.

With the creator they were one
And with the world he made.
But jealous was your heart,
Resentment, discord growing wild.
Feeling cast out and abandoned
You craved to be like them ...
But it was not to be,
For God's curse adorned your brow.

For this reason, and only this,
You turned away and tried
To find the world
That God withheld from you
By flight from soul and self.
With words of simple unison,
Telling of joyous simplicity,
Of submission to destiny,
Of the course of time and season
And the value in the smallness,
There you hoped to find
What was banned from you.

Yet as the clock of life
The last hours began to chime,
You knew indeed
That despite, despite, despite
The hardship, unspeakable hardship
Of your endless struggles,
That despite the scars from forge's fire
And despite the bitter cold of bearing pain
Of self-denial and self-failing,

THE DEATH OF ADALBERT STIFTER

Nothingness, emptiness and guilt alone
Must end your earthly days.

Amelie was betrayal!
And Gustav Heckenast a foe.
Good old Aprent was a stranger.
Brother Anton was a sham,
And so also Kirchschlag, Oberplan
And Linz,
Not heaven, but hell and destruction.

And so only one remained:
His name was Death!
Will he now give you
What life was withholding?
Will he lead you now
To some new dawning
Where the dew of mercy
Soothes your waiting eyes?

And as the cry
Of tormenting terror
Had faded far away,
As with it too your waking soul
Had taken pain and misery,
Then an image grew:
You saw yourself.
Barefoot you stood
And lightly clothed
On a winter's night so harsh
And deep in snow:
Repentant and hungry too,
Yet proud, not bent –
A gate before you.
It was Tuscany,

Enshrouded with wintery grip.
To repent was your intent
Yet you were from repentance
Far removed.

You needed help,
But this was mere desire;
You wanted mercy,
But you could not revere;
Despite all, you strove
But found no end.

Adalbert Stifter,
A voice did sound!
Do you know your Canossa?
Adalbert Stifter,
Do you know your need?
Destruction you must find
Before you newly rise!
You must wither
To find yourself anew,
Be lost
Before you can unite
With God and church
And with the Good on earth.

But now the very essence of your words
Lives in so many human hearts.
They encourage peace
That you had been denied,
They nurture faith
That you could never find,
They offer solace too
That you had been denied.
And those three: Faith, Solace, Peace

Rise upwards now
And warm your soul,
Enlighten your spirit,
And offer healing there
Where heavenly light and joy
Surround you.

Oh, become once more a human
And come,
Descend to earth again!
Find here
The Word and also Mercy
From the Christ himself.

Oh, have once more the courage
For being human.
And all that was so wrong
Will Good become.

Transformation

In dying
Human breath widens
Into the whole of cosmic widths.
The Word
Takes off to rise
On wings of breath
Eagle-like towards the sun,
The Word of human soul.
The human form it falls to ash
Out of eagle-breath-wings
To earth below.

In birth
Human breath flows
With the first gasp
Into the body's sheaths.
With wings of breath
The Thought of gods
– *The human being* –
Descends from moon's silvery realms
To the earth body below.

It finds its way
Through crystal-weaving
That shapes the human head.
The salt of bodily life
Is filled and flows to become

The Thought of gods
— *The human being* —
That, which was Word,
Had been lost to cosmic heights
In death,
Now it comes as Thought
Back once more
Through birth.

The angels carried me
As I once died,
And through my life and path
Had I defiled and deformed the Word.
Yet the angels carried this poor,
Fragmented, shattered Word
Up towards the heavenly realm.
There came all hierarchies
And transformed the ailing Word,
Healing, making whole once more
That which had been ruined.
This transformed, healthy Word
Flowed as the Thought I now was,
As my Thought-self
To earth again. And
I was born.

From my limbs
This Word flows in death —
From my hands,
My feet,
From arm and leg,
Shoulder and thigh,
From spine
And muscles, from my fibres,
From joints,

From bones and blood,
From organs which once
Gave me life
From their light and force.
But there, where I in life
Have failed,
There, where I had prompted
Death and destruction
Through wrong action
And wrongful will,
Through harmful word
And untrue deeds
Through vanity and grudge,
The forming forces of the limbs
And the creative form of body
Became then ill and poor.
All this
My angel took.
He offered it
To realms of higher beings.
Archai and Kyriotetes received
And Mights and Powers carried
Into their realms
The ill and deformed Word
That had become untrue.

There my fingers once more
Became straight and free
Through the forming rays.
The hierarchies
They arched again
The arches of my feet
And palms of my hands.
They formed the forces of my blood
And the life of my organs

TRANSFORMATION

To become the new form
Of my head
That is itself a parable.
Arm by arm
And leg by leg,
My body is transformed
My ear was shaped,
And the roundness of my eye.
The skull became a dome
And the jaws stretched
Their strength into gestalt.
Body was now head.
From the Word the Thought was formed.

The planetary spheres
And starry paths let flow
Their blessings into me.
The stars now danced their course
Within my being.
Then flowed my becoming
Into my gift of thinking.
Body was now head,
The Word transformed
To force of Thought.
Birth had come to pass
And placed me into earthly house.

This earthly dwelling
Filled itself
With heavy load
And molecules
Gathered around the earthly home,
Stone and waters
All the weighty powers.
And so the hierarchies' building-work

Became earthly body-form.
Crystals found their stone,
Salt transformed with ashes.
Weaving light became earthly weight.
Phantom disappeared ...
Body in its place.

This body now I bear
Through all my earthly days.
I know it will
At life's end
Be dispersed
And from its very parts,
Its ruins,
Wounds and scars,
The gods with all their grace
Will gather up once more
The image of themselves.
Body will be head
And the Word transformed
To be the Thought.

In you, O Christ,
The body could become the head.
Through your grace
Your love
Your all-embracing
Power of mercy
Could ash become
Salt of the earth.

Your head,
It became the resurrection.
Your head,
It was sacrifice,

And became
The lamb of the world.
Since then
We all can die
Into your love.
The Lamb of God
It holds
The resurrection flag.
You are the Lamb of God,
Your spirit is
The resurrection flag.

But now my eye
May see you
And melt
In the sight
Of your mercy.

III

Birth and Death

Essays

4

The Experience of Birth and Death in Childhood

In his book *Knowledge of the Higher Worlds,* Rudolf Steiner describes certain experiences which the human soul undergoes in training to gain knowledge of realms beyond the sense-perceptible. A psychologist will find on almost every page descriptions they have encountered in dealing with patients, when analysing their problems or explaining their dreams. If even a few of the exercises given in this book are done, gradually a certain amount of clarity is reached as to the boundaries between conscious and unconscious, which were not known or recognised before. It is not necessary to achieve clairvoyance. The mere fact of trying to educate our own thinking, to unfold our emotional life under self-control, and to exercise our volition, makes the human soul into an ordered instrument which is gradually tuned to such an extent that harmony and not discord rules it.

In preparing the soul to reach, in full consciousness, the borders of the unconscious, we experience, at the gate which leads down into this realm, two special emotions. They are more than mere emotions, however. They are the two archetypes of human emotional life.

We are all constantly filled by them, although they are very well hidden, and in balanced people seldom shoot up to the surface of the mind. These two primary emotions, or rather elementary soul-experiences, are fear and shame.

Fear, with all its varied possibilities – fear of death and fear of dogs; fear of parents and the fear of being shut into a closed room (claustrophobia); fear of crossing a street, of entering a house; fear of the dark and fear of infection.

Shame, with all its implications – shame of being stripped and shame of being spoken to; shame at having to appear in a gathering of people; shame appearing as modesty, and shame disguised as bashfulness.

These two experiences are like two guardians constantly watching the gate that bars the way from the conscious to the unconscious. They are always present, always awake, and readily appear if the gate should be opened by an unprepared mind, or shaken from its hinges by outer events. Although brothers, fear and shame are in themselves as different as day from night. The bashfulness of a young person and the fear of a terror-stricken culprit are poles apart.

If we experience fear, we are overcome by a feeling of cold, of tightness, of oppression. It is as if some unknown force had thrown belts of iron round our chest, neck, and heart. We feel sometimes unable to move, rooted to the spot; our life is frozen, our will under a spell.

Shame is different: we are not held tight but rather feel limp, as though all our strength were draining away. In shame, also, we feel quite unable to act, but this impotency is entirely different from the incapacity we experience with fear. To feel ashamed means to feel helpless, given up to surrounding circumstances – loose, not tight; limp, not rigid. We wish to disappear in the helplessness of our plight – 'Oh, if only the earth would swallow me up!' The person haunted by fear has the desire to run away and is unable to do so. The person gripped by shame has no power to run away either; he can only slip away.

4. THE EXPERIENCE OF BIRTH AND DEATH IN CHILDHOOD

Shame and fear were experienced by Adam and Eve as soon as they had eaten of the Tree of Knowledge. 'Then the eyes of them both were opened, and they realised they were naked.'

To know that we are 'naked' is the fundamental meaning behind the experience of shame. Therefore all shame, bashfulness, and even modesty, have an emotional background of guilt. That we are here on earth, human beings, children parted from the Great Mother, and that all this has happened through our own fault – all these feelings lie behind the experience of shame. Therefore we try to cover our nakedness, and we blush. In blushing we cover this naked existence, though not very successfully.

> They hid from the LORD God among the trees of the garden. But the LORD God called to the man, 'Where are you?'
> He answered, 'I heard you in the garden, and I was afraid because I was naked; so I hid.'

In these few verses from Genesis (3:7–10) it is clearly stated that Adam and Eve first experienced shame. As long as the guilt of the Fall is hidden, shame is the result. As soon as the guilt appears, in the image of God the Father, shame changes into fear, for in this moment death hovers above Adam and Eve. This the devil had not told them: that although they would become as God, knowing good and evil, they would have to pay for their knowledge with the coin of death.

Human souls are not permitted to experience their nakedness – for instance, their clarity of mind and their consciousness – without paying for it with death. Shame may guard the threshold, and we may forget that we have to pay for our 'nakedness'. Fear makes us aware that death is round the corner at every moment of our existence.

The indecision and uncertainty of modern psychology, and the possibility of interpreting almost everything into anything in psychoanalysis, are the result of a complete inability to coordinate psychic experiences with bodily processes. In the last edition (1947) of Flanders Dunbar's standard book, *Emotions and Bodily Changes*, 2,400 books and papers are quoted in the reference list, all dealing with psychosomatic facts. A wealth of information is given about the possible ways in which mental conditions can influence the body and vice versa. In spite of this, it is not possible yet to describe scientifically how and or in what way mental processes can penetrate and directly bring about a change in the bodily nature of man and animal.

If we look for references to fear and shame in this book we shall not find them. If we search for scientific descriptions of the actual bodily place where fear and shame are experienced, we shall do so in vain. Nevertheless, fear and shame leave deep impressions on the body, and we should be able to locate the seat of their activities.

Within our bodies are two different and opposite layers: the blood and the nervous system. The blood is a continuously flowing fluid and the nerves an ever-resting structure. The blood is the fluid which is constantly destroyed and renewed again. The short lifespan of blood cells is a conspicuous feature of this special fluid. The nerve, be it cell or fibre, once built, remains throughout our lifetime, hardly altered within the body.

Flaming red is the colour of blood; pale yellow the tinge of nerves. Warmth is the nature of blood and coolness the quality of nerves. Blood has its centre in the heart, from which it flows and to which it returns. The nerve, on the other hand, has its centre in the central nervous system, from which thousands of nerve-fibres reach their different organs. Blood is a never-ceasing continuum; the nerve, a fixed structure of space.

4. THE EXPERIENCE OF BIRTH AND DEATH IN CHILDHOOD

The central nervous system, brain and spinal cord, lie firmly enclosed in the cave of the skull and the spinal column. There they are enshrined and communicate with the different parts of the body by means of the nerves. The small holes through which the nerves reach out to their bodily environment, to all its different organs, are like embrasures. The whole central nervous system is like a body within the body, kept apart by the skull and the spine. Seen in an imaginative way, the brain and spinal cord have withdrawn from the remaining part of the body into a kind of splendid isolation. The blood is different. Its central organ, the heart, has not withdrawn from the body but rather lies in the middle of it. It communicates with the body by a continuous giving and taking.

Quite evidently, most of the experiences of the soul that reach consciousness are connected with a properly functioning nervous system. Sense-perception, the forming of concepts, emotions and voluntary actions are all bound up with the nerves. The lower we descend into the animal kingdom, the less complexity do we find in the nervous structure. 'Progressive cerebration' as it is called, the progressive enlargement of the brain through evolution in the animal kingdom, leads to the development of consciousness.

Not so readily found is the bodily location of the unconscious. There is no proper place in our body to which it can be ascribed. The sympathetic nervous system, with all its ramifications, may be thought of in this connection. It influences our breathing, our heart-beat, the tension of our blood vessels, the functions of most of our organs. Yet this sympathetic nervous system is part of the whole complex of nerves, and therefore serves our conscious soul-experience.

Our higher sense-organs (the retina in the eye, the cochlea in the ear) are guarded by a system of intermediaries whose task is to shield the organ from the full impact of the outer world – think of the lens and iris of the eye, or of the drum and ossicles of the middle ear. Colours and sounds are sifted by these special organs.

Such is the task of the sympathetic nervous system with regard to the brain and the spinal cord. It shields the organ of consciousness from the experience of our inner emotions. We should never be able to experience our surroundings in an unbiased way if the sympathetic nerves did not put up a barrier against our emotions, our feelings, our passions. Our sense-organs would be flooded with our subjective experiences and we should be entirely consumed by hate and sympathy, by antipathy and desire. The fact that our brain remains cool, and that we are able to judge not only according to our subjective emotions but also according to our objective opinions, we owe to the sympathetic nerves. This system of nerves creates a barrier round our consciousness and has the task of preventing the inner world of our unconscious from penetrating it.

We may accordingly suggest that the whole of our sympathetic nervous system forms the most complicated gate between the conscious and the unconscious. The unconscious itself, therefore, lies beyond this gate, and its place is none other than in the ocean of the blood. Bound up with the life of our blood is the unconscious realm of the soul. This means that the human being, as an eternal being, is connected with the blood of its body, and only part of its being rises up into its conscious experience. Those of our inner experiences which are sifted through the sympathetic nervous system reach our consciousness. Everything else remains in the dark, bound to the blood. What analytical psychology calls the 'collective psyche' is to be found in this realm. There live the archetypes with all their manifold ramifications. The whole, hidden wealth of our soul's existence, unknown to us, is there.

Analytical psychology has also shown that even in earliest childhood these archetypes are present, and known to the

4. THE EXPERIENCE OF BIRTH AND DEATH IN CHILDHOOD

child. In his book *The Life of Childhood,* Michael Fordham writes: 'The fundamental idea behind this book is that the child starts life with a psyche that is not known to them, but through which they grow and become conscious.' This, Dr. Fordham shows; but he never ventures to ask the question, where does this psyche come from with which we all start life?

The sea of the blood holds the 'collective psyche', and the whole of the nervous system gradually brings part of the psyche into our consciousness. Blood and nerves are part of our body, and our body we receive from our mother. The psyche itself is ours, and there is no other possibility but to accept the fact that the soul unites with the body at a certain moment during the embryonic development, or gradually during this embryonic time and the time of earliest childhood.

This process of unification of body and soul is a twofold one. The soul unites with the blood and also with the nerves. The part of the soul's being which unites with the blood remains unconscious; or it may manifest, especially in early childhood, in the form of 'projections' out into the world of the child's dreams. The growing consciousness frees itself from these projections and gradually learns to distinguish the world around from the life within.

There are some reports about this; one of them, from the autobiography of H.M. Stanley, may be quoted.

> My personal recollections do not extend beyond the time I lay in the cradle. Up to a certain date in the early [eighteen-]forties, all is profound darkness to me. Then, as I awoke from sleep one day, a brief period of consciousness suddenly dawned upon my faculties. There was an indefinable murmur about me, some unintelligible views floated before my senses, light flashed upon the spirit and I entered into being.

At what age I first received these dim but indelible impressions, I cannot guess. It must have been in helpless infancy, for I seem to have passed, subsequently, through a long age of dreams, wherein countless vague experiences, emotions, and acts occurred which, though indefinable, left shadowy traces on my memory. During such a mechanical stage of existence, it was not possible for me to distinguish between dreams and realities.

I fancy I see a white ceiling, and square joists, with meat hooks attached to them, a round, pink, human face, the frill of a cap, a bit of bright ribbon; but before I am able to grasp the meaning of what I see, I have lapsed into unconsciousness again. After an immeasurable time, the faculties seem to be reawakened, and I can distinguish tones, and am aware that I can see, hear, and feel, and that I am in my cradle. It is close by a wooden staircase, and my eyes follow its length up, and then down: I catch sight of a housefly, and then another, and their buzz and movements become absorbing. Presently a woman advances, bends over me a moment, then lifts me up in her arms, and from a great height I survey my world.

There is a settle of dark wood, a bit of carving at the end of it; there is a black, shiny chimney; a red coal fire, with one spluttering jet of flame, and waving soot flakes: there is a hissing black kettle, and a thread of vapour from the nozzle; a curious old clock, with intensely red flowers above and chains and weights below it; and lastly I see a door cut into two halves, the upper one being wide open, through which I gain my first view of sky and space. This last is a sight worth seeing, and I open my eyes roundly to take stock of this pearly space and its drifting fleece as seen through the door, and my attention is divided between the sky and the tick-tock of the clock, while forced to speculate what the white day and the pearly void mean.

4. THE EXPERIENCE OF BIRTH AND DEATH IN CHILDHOOD

There follows a transition into another state of conscious being wherein I appear to have wings, and to be soaring up to the roof of a great hall, and sailing from corner to corner, like a humming bee on a tour of exploration; and the roof presently being removed, I launch out with wings outspread, joyous and free, until I lose myself in the unknowable, to emerge, some time after, in my own cradle-nest at the foot of the wooden stairs.

And thus for an unknown stretch of time, I endure my days without apparent object, but quietly observant, and an inarticulate witness of a multitude of small events; and thus I waited and watched and dreamed, surrendering myself to my state, undisturbed, unaffected, unresisting, borne along by Time until I could stand and take a larger and more deliberate survey of the strange things done around me.

Quite often, in the recollections of well-known people, there appear, in earliest childhood, these moments, when the dawn of the conscious experience of the world around is recorded in almost minute detail. These memories are like small islands in the sea of the time of childhood. It is as if the panorama of dreams and projections is broken by these islands, until gradually they merge together and become a conscious perception of the surrounding world.

When we are born we first have to cross the River of Life, the flow of blood. Our soul enters the house of the body and gradually merges with the organs. The soul enters the blood, but it also permeates the nerves, and these two experiences are entirely different in character. To describe it in an appropriate way we would have to say that we die into the ocean of our blood, and are gradually born in the realm of our nerves.

The death in the blood brings about the experience of oblivion. We forget everything that was known to us before we were born. We lived in a world beyond space, and now we die into the river of time, the blood. Part of our soul gradually emerges from this drowned existence and takes hold of the world which is opened to us by our senses, and this, when later recalled, forms our first memories.

The experience of oblivion by drowning in the blood is the first experience of death in childhood. The dawn of consciousness by means of our senses and nerves is the first experience of birth. Some of us are able to remember the latter; the former we can make only indirectly accessible. I shall refer to this indirect way presently.

The birth into the outer environment by means of our nerves is accompanied by a constant experience of shame. The death into the blood is accompanied by fear. Fear is the soul's attribute when it stands in front of death, and death to the soul means departure, forgetting itself, dismembering itself. Shame is the soul's quality when it stands before cognition. Cognition means birth to the soul; it means to remember, to know, to experience consciously.

The child establishes its life in the tension of these two emotions. The soul is drowned in the blood to experience the world of space and earth. By this process our unconscious is created. The soul reawakens through the nerves to comprehend the world of space and earth by means of the sense-organs. Thus our conscious experiences are born. At the shore of the river of blood, there stands eternal shame. At the border of the land of nerves perpetual fear stalks. Fear and shame close the gate between the two realms during the soul's life on earth.

Fear is the guardian who keeps the gate closed from the side of consciousness. As soon as the unconscious tries to break through into conscious existence, fear rises up and consciousness harnesses all its powers to ward off the attack. Shame is the guardian who keeps the gate closed from the side of the unconscious. As soon as consciousness tries to

4. THE EXPERIENCE OF BIRTH AND DEATH IN CHILDHOOD

invade the unconscious realm, shame comes into action. Shame inhabits the blood and fear inhabits the nerves. If the nerves try to attack the blood, shame appears. If the blood tries to overwhelm the nerves, fear comes into action.

In many forms and variations, the descent of the human soul into the body is described in fairy tales. When a fairy tale speaks about two children, it is describing these two parts of the soul which, after birth, unite respectively with blood and nerve. *Hansel and Gretel, Little Brother and Little Sister, Jorinde and Joringel*, are only a few examples.

In Hansel and Gretel the two children enter the dark wood and finally reach the house of the witch. So the soul leaves the spirit world, enters on its way towards earth existence, and at last finds its body. Hungry after their long journey, the children eat parts of the witch's house, until she appears and imprisons them both. Hansel is put into a cage and Gretel has to serve in the house. The human soul is put into the cage of the head and brain to gain experience of the outer world, and it has to serve the body by being drowned in the blood. Therefore, Hansel is well fed, whereas Gretel is starved.

This lasts for a certain time until the witch is ready to put Hansel into the oven and eat him. Gretel, however, is clever enough to throw the witch into the oven. Then she opens Hansel's cage and both are free again. They gather the witch's treasures, gold and precious stones, and return to their father enriched and happy. In death the human soul frees itself from the grip of the witch and returns to the spirit realm with the experiences (treasures) gained on earth.

In *Little Brother and Little Sister* the same thing is described in a different way. The brother, thirsting for a drink, succumbs to his desire and is turned into a little fawn. He represents that part of the soul which drowns in the blood. His sister takes him with her to live in a house in the wood. The sister represents the part of the soul which gradually grows conscious, being enshrined in the house of the brain. There they live until the king of the country appears upon the scene. The king represents something new, those spiritual powers which can awaken within the conscious part of the soul to lead us to gain higher experiences than those of the senses. The marriage of Little Sister and the king takes place, but Little Brother must remain a fawn and his enchantment is broken only when his Sister, the conscious part of the soul, has suffered the probations and trials on the way to higher knowledge.

In these stories we are able to behold true images that mostly remain hidden when speaking about the soul. The human soul has a twofold existence here on earth, the conscious part and the unconscious one. Although they are parted, they belong together, like two lovers unable to reach one another. Romeo and Juliet we may call them, or Hero and Leander, or any of the names which appear in mythology related to the same realm.

Each part of the soul has a companion. In the conscious part it takes the form of a dog, and this is fear; in the unconscious it takes the form of a hare. This is shame. In childhood, as well as in later life, we are continually accompanied by these two figures. The mythologies of dog and hare, if studied thoroughly, will confirm this statement.

The child's soul, having gone through the first experiences of birth and death, has gained certain qualities which from then onwards are available to it. Children know death in its inner meaning, and birth is not foreign to them. Wherever they come into contact with the world, the ideas of birth and death are applied to it. It is therefore not surprising that in 1937 a child psychologist, Mlle Thomas, observed that two thirds of children, on being asked to complete a certain story, referred in their answers to death or dying, to killing and parting.[1] Mlle Thomas was surprised by this unexpected result, though she might have

4. THE EXPERIENCE OF BIRTH AND DEATH IN CHILDHOOD

known that death is a common subject in the fantasy-life of childhood. Therefore, it is a bit ridiculous of many teachers and doctors to instruct parents not to tell gruesome fairy tales to their children and to avoid mentioning death and dying. Whether we do so or not, children know at least as much as we do about death. Their soul has died in its blood, and they know the horror and pain involved.

Sylvia Anthony made the following comment:

> How does the child think about death in their fantasies, if one of their family has actually died recently?
>
> ... There may then be no mention of death at all, but the idea of guilt may assume obsessional proportions in the content of the child's thought. They may express a fear of imprisonment, and see every misfortune of themselves or anyone else as a just punishment, from which they assume that they have been guilty of some crime, although they may have no idea what the crime could be.[2]

Professor David and Rosa Katz, in their *Conversations with Children,* wrote:

> We tried in every way to keep from our children the idea of the death of people, and we believe that a similar reticence is common to most parents ... It is true that in fairy tales there is a great deal – indeed too much – about striking dead, burning to death ... but the child does not comprehend what really lies behind it. For the child, death in fairy tales, probably means nothing more than 'not playing any longer', the withdrawal of the person concerned. Our children also spoke quite often about murder and shooting in the shallow sense just mentioned.

85

Sylvia Anthony, who quotes this passage, adds, 'But only the last sentence gives evidence of the children's actual behaviour. Whatever death may have meant to these children, it certainly was not absent from their thoughts.'

This is a correct statement. Children have some inherent knowledge of death, with all its implications. They have experienced death as a means of being alive here on earth.

I shall quote from another autobiography, a narrative which, in this respect, is most illuminating. Isolde Kurz wrote:

> During the same time I made another shattering discovery. One day, in gazing out of the window I saw a group of men, clothed in black, passing by. They were carrying something wrapped in black cloth, which appeared to me to be a big trunk. This sight touched me painfully, and Christine, our new nursemaid, in answering my question, said it was a corpse, which the men were carrying to the cemetery.
>
> 'What is a corpse?' I asked, with disgust, for I had never heard the word before and it sounded strange and gruesome.
>
> She answered by saying that it was a dead man. I was astonished that human beings should die, for I had always thought that death was a bad accident, which happened only to birds, dogs, cats, and such beasts. Christine tried to lead me away from these thoughts, but I would not be led and ran to my mother, crying, 'Is it true that people die?'
>
> 'Who told you so?'
>
> 'Christine.' I at once discovered that Christine had broken a commandment.
>
> 'Poor darling!' my mother said, 'you should not have been told for a long time, but now it is done. Yes, it is true, people have to die!'

4. THE EXPERIENCE OF BIRTH AND DEATH IN CHILDHOOD

'But certainly not everyone, mummy?'
'Yes, child, everyone!' She kept me in her arms as if she wanted to console me.
'But not you, mummy?'
'Yes, I also, child.'
'But not daddy?'
'Yes, daddy also.'
'Then perhaps I also?'
'Yes, you also, but not for a long, long time to come.'
The long time of which she spoke was no consolation to me. A fearful, black abyss yawned, which swallowed up everything.

This is the typical story of the rediscovery of death in early childhood, experienced in the realm of consciousness. It is nothing new to the child. The sight of the coffin, although she did not know what it was, touched her painfully. She still wanted to suppress what her unconscious told her, and therefore Christine, the maid, had to perform the task which the child herself was afraid to undertake. This is the rediscovery of death. She would never have understood the impact of her experience if she herself had not known beforehand what death is in reality – forgetting, dissolving, parting.

This experience of death can appear also in other forms. The great German dramatist, Friedrich Hebbel, wrote in his autobiography, *Meine Kindheit,* a mine of information for every psychologist:

> I could not endure seeing a bone, and buried even the smallest one which could be found in our little garden. Later I even erased the word 'rib' from the Catechism with my nails, because it suggested this nauseous thing so vividly that I could visualise a rotting cadaver.

These quotations could be enlarged by very many other examples. They all show one thing: children have an inborn knowledge of death due to their first experience, for birth is the death of the soul into the blood of the body.

I have tried to propose, in this short study of the child's experience of birth and death, that these two experiences are common to every human being from earliest childhood upwards, and that the outer birth of the body, the release from the motherly womb, involves a double experience, the death of the soul in the blood and the birth of the soul in the perception of the outer world, through the nerves and sensory organs. Thus the two realms of our mental life on earth are created – the gradual unfolding of our conscious mind and the establishment of the unconscious. Both are a fundamental experience of human life here on earth.

A last word should be said about those two emotional qualities, fear and shame, which guard the threshold between the conscious and the unconscious mind. I said that fear inhabits our nerves, guarding the conscious realm from the intrusions of the unconscious. What then is fear? Leo Kanner, in his book, *Child Psychiatry,* wrote:

> Watson was the first to study, experimentally, the emotional responses of infants during the first months of life. He found that from the very day of birth they reacted to a group of situations in a mode which impressed the observer as being an indication of fear. Sudden catching of the breath, clutching randomly with the hands, sudden closing of the eye-lids, puckering of the lips and then crying.
>
> ... The meaning of the term 'fear' implies the idea of existing or anticipated danger, as well as the individual's attitude in the face of such danger. There are other sets of facts which, in spite of their resemblance to the combination alluded to as 'fear', show sufficient

4. THE EXPERIENCE OF BIRTH AND DEATH IN CHILDHOOD

dissimilarity to have warranted the creation of other names, such as 'apprehension', 'dread', 'fright', 'terror', 'horror', 'alarm', 'consternation', etc.

In this quotation, two fundamental qualities of fear are stated. First, that fear is present from almost the first day of human life, onwards. Secondly, that fear is a special reaction of the soul, different from dread, fright, and so on. But just these latter reactions, which Kanner quotes, are born in the soul when faced with danger. Fear, true fear, is not caused directly by the threat of danger. If we have to face a dangerous situation, the gate of the threshold is crushed by the unconscious, and this crushing, not the danger, creates fear. Then we turn pale, feel tense, sweat all over, our breath is arrested, and our conscious perceptions are raised to the highest pitch. It is as if the conscious part of the soul, having concentrated all its powers and resources, had been inhaled entirely into the nervous part of the body. The valves between blood and sympathetic nerves are shut. A oneness of soul and nervous system is created.

The opposite experience is shame. Sir Arthur Mitchell wrote:

> The state of the mind during a blush, described broadly, is one of confusion, and this is often strongly marked. 'Covered with confusion,' indeed, is a way of describing persons who are in the act of blushing. Darwin says that they 'lose their presence of mind, and utter singularly inappropriate remarks. They are often distressed, stammer and make awkward movements and strange grimaces.' This excellently describes their confusion. Excessive blushers do not rightly know what they are saying and *feel* stupid.

Quoting Francis Bacon, he writes further:

> Bacon says: 'Shame causeth blushing and casting down of the eyes,' and there is not much more than this to be said about the cause and character of blushing. It consists of a 'resort of blood to the face with a casting down of the eyes' arising out of a sense of shame ...
>
> If I am asked to define with sharpness and shortness the meaning of the word shame, as the word which best names the cause of blushing, I confess that I cannot do so, nor have I found any other person able to furnish such a definition.

The experience of shame creates in the body this very peculiar symptom of blushing, the casting down of the eyes and the confused state of mind. These are signs exactly opposite to those of fear. In fear, we turn pale; we widen the eyes in a sense of horror, and the mind is fixed and entirely clear. This shows that when feeling ashamed the subconscious part of the soul loosens its grip on the blood, and the blood therefore rises up into the face; the mind is blurred for a short time and the eyes are cast down, because the comprehension of the world is withdrawn. A process of exhaling takes place within the unconscious part of the soul, which is trying to overcome the conscious mind. If we were able to state that fear is an inhaling of the soul into the nervous system, we can now add that shame is an exhaling of the soul from the blood.

It is well-known that in indigenous people whose normal state is nakedness, the blush is extended over almost the whole body. Not only neck and face, but also the chest, the arms, and sometimes even the thighs blush. To me this is a sign which establishes the statement that shame is the state of mind in which we experience our 'nakedness'. The soul tries to hide this 'nakedness' and blushing occurs. The

4. THE EXPERIENCE OF BIRTH AND DEATH IN CHILDHOOD

feeling of 'nakedness' is rooted in the idea that someone in our surroundings is able to see our faults, has uncovered our sins. Thus Mitchell said, 'In the sense of shame that raises a blush, conscience plays little or no part. It is not the feeling of guilt, but the thought that others think us guilty.'

In shame we experience our own nakedness, a condition of being 'given up' to the eyes of others. In fear we experience our own guilt and the result of it, the necessity of death.

If this statement is correct, then every human soul, by experiencing fear and shame, carries within itself the last remnants of the eternal shock which man experienced with the Fall. The implications of the original sin, described in the Bible in the image of eating of the fruit from the Tree of Knowledge, are still experienced when we feel ashamed or frightened.

Shame is the repercussion of the moment when Adam and Eve discovered their nakedness. Fear is the repercussion of the other moment when they learned that death is the result of the awareness of nakedness. Through the Fall, the human soul was able gradually to be born in the nervous system. This birth into earthly surroundings, by the opening of the eyes, is necessarily accompanied by shame. The consequence is the necessity to experience death, and this is accompanied by fear.

The human soul exhales when ashamed and inhales when afraid, and is thus able to establish the conscious part as well as the unconscious. As every human being is endowed with these two emotions, we are all under the spell of the original sin, the Fall.

It was through Christ that the redemption of the Fall was initiated. Only by accepting him into the life of the human soul can shame and fear be overcome.

5

The Moment of Death Within the Yearly and Daily Rhythm

Recently medical science has attached increasingly more significance to the circumstances of weather and seasons in connection to particular illnesses. A year ago an extensive study by De Rudder was published, giving a synopsis of the exact data as researched to date. Since this publication more and more articles have appeared in medical journals with additional observations in this field. The aim of this article is to point out just one of the many phenomena that have been discovered.

In his book De Rudder presents the average monthly number of deaths in the years 1923 and 1924 in Germany, showing that there was a significant peak of mortality in the months of January, February and March. De Rudder expresses it in the following way: 'The total mortality in civilisations of the northern temperate zone shows a distinct increase in late winter and early spring' (p. 93).

On account of these observations Professor Hagentorn published his research results in 1932 about the connection of illness to weather conditions and included a chart showing the frequency of deaths in relation to the time of day and night. The peak of mortality is to be found in the early hours between 2.00 am and 5.00 am. I find Professor Hagentorn's comment on this of such importance that I would like to quote him:

> It is particularly evident that human mortality reaches a culmination in spring, moreover in early spring, although one could have assumed that late autumn should have shown itself to be the peak of mortality, as it is undoubtably the most malevolent season according to human experience. Now it becomes apparent that this is not the case. Mortality increases with January and February, with biological spring, and peaks in March and April. To give an explanation for this is difficult. The most probable seems to lie in the assumption of a specific effect of spring air, and involuntarily a comparison to the periodicity during daytime hours presents itself, due to the fact that mortality also peaks in the early morning hours. Not in autumn and winter and not in the night, but early spring and the early morning seem to be the times when the most people die. *Spring, particularly early spring, could then be seen as the early morning hours of the year.*[1]

A few sentences previously Hagentorn had wanted to ascribe the seasonal concentration of human mortality to a certain effect of spring air, but then he suddenly arrived at the idea of calling early spring the 'early morning hours of the year'. Why both of these two time periods are simultaneously the peak of mortality, of course he cannot explain; he does, however, notice the significance of the comparison and with it strikes exactly the right cord.

Rudolf Steiner was able to describe, for the first time in modern language, how the whole being of the earth is subject to sublime processes of respiration that take place throughout the cycle of the year as well as in the rhythm of day and night. And we cannot mistake the fact that the soul of the earth, in exhaling with the springtime as well as every morning, entices human beings to use this helping hand for their own process of exhaling into death. It is as if the living being of the earth takes the human soul onto its wings when the body exhales the soul with its last breath, and in this way helps it in its ascent from earthly life.

Hagentorn indicates correctly that one would actually expect a higher death rate in autumn because at this time of year there is a strong rise in the number of illnesses. Therefore he cannot explain why it is just the springtime, when everything starts to come to life again, that the most deaths occur.

Continuing this research, Professor Fischer from the University of Rostock published statistics about mortality in connection to the time of day.[2] Here also the peak of the curve is to be found in the early morning hours, between 2.00 am and 6.00 am. A second, smaller peak was around midday.

Also this work confirms the earlier research. When the earth exhales, whether it be the daily or annual breath, in the early morning or in early spring, it is more able to carry the human soul that is waiting to be released from the body with it into the spirit world than at any other time. Without knowledge of the breathing process of the earth the charts would remain mere insignificant and unintelligible lines. It will be of importance time and again in future to become aware of such subtle phenomena described by today's exact sciences. In this way the thoughts Rudolf Steiner that presented can come to fruition.

The following chart illustrates the above account by gathering together all previous statistical data. The relationship of annual mortality to the occurrence of death within the diurnal rhythm is clearly shown.

5. THE MOMENT OF DEATH WITHIN THE YEARLY AND DAILY RHYTHM

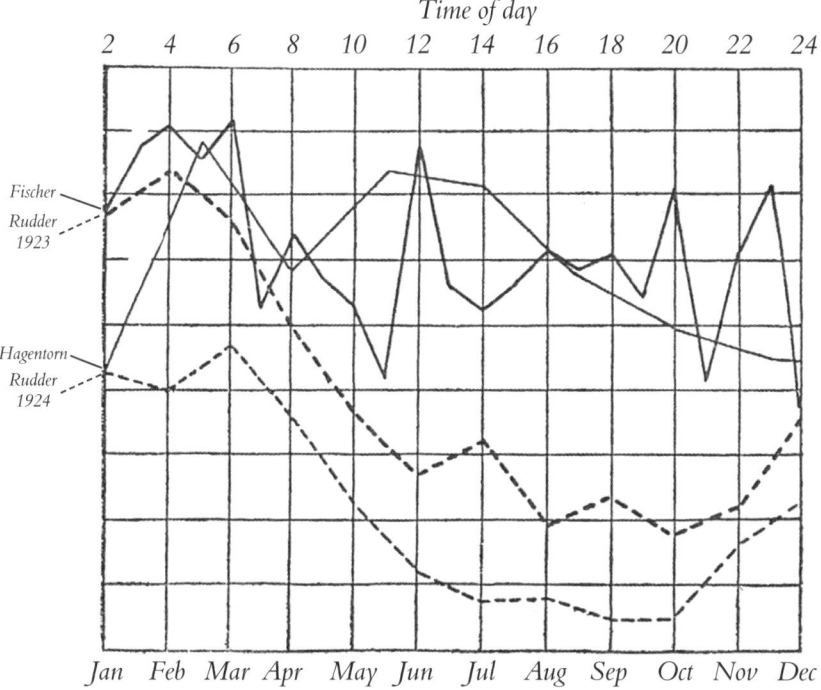

Chart comparing Rudder, Hagentorn and Fischer's annual and diurnal death rates.

In his book De Rudder has a graph showing the seasonal occurrence of scarlet fever and diphtheria in the United States over a nine-year period. This clearly shows that both diseases have their seasonal peak in the deep winter season. In fact, diphtheria always peaks in December and scarlet fever in January.

Both diseases have a consistent peak. One could almost say that scarlet fever is always on diphtheria's heels. Furthermore, there is an interdependence of these two diseases expressed by the fact that when diphtheria diseases decline, an increase in scarlet fever follows, and when diphtheria disease is frequent, a decrease in scarlet fever is observed.

The peak of both of these diseases lies in the deep winter

period, precisely the time of year in which humans rely entirely on themselves.

The earth has breathed in and as spiritual beings humans have completely withdrawn into themselves.

In a lecture on the seasonal festivals Rudolf Steiner spoke about the fact that in the old mysteries the words, 'Beware of evil,' were called to people especially at this time of year.[3]

These two diseases are certainly diseases that affect the innermost human being within us. This is something Rudolf Steiner has said a lot about in particular.[4] Scarlet fever is the deepest confrontation that the human being as a child has with their inherited body. Rudolf Steiner states that the causes of diphtheria are to be found in a previous life on earth. Both diseases are intimately connected, which is also shown by the fact that the symptoms of diphtheria can often be present in the beginning of scarlet fever.

Professor Hagentorn also makes a characteristic comparison by saying, 'Is the diphtheria-scarlet fever relationship not a completely analogous phenomenon to the one we observe in the plant world, namely that lilac regularly blooms before jasmine?'[5]

Such remarks give the impression that the author is inwardly apologizing to his colleagues, but only because he feels that an archetypal phenomenon, which he can barely grasp, has come to his mind in an imaginative way, even though he cannot find a rational explanation for it. But whoever learns to look at human beings as Rudolf Steiner taught us, will find the clue to a chronobiology of illness in just such a comparison. Just as humans stand in the midst of the kingdoms of nature and are partly devoted to the rhythm of the earth and the cosmos, so too diseases surround them as a kingdom of their own and, depending on the time of year, manifest themselves in a similar way to plants that only bloom one after another.

Appendix

1. Preparatory notes for a lecture about death, 1947

Lecture, Leeds, October 27th 1947

(The Problem of Death)

I.
1.) Death as problem of our time.
   Everywhere it is Death which surrounds us & meets.
2.) Have we really considered the "Problem of Death"? Have we studied its implications?
3.) From a biological & medical point of view I shall try & deal with the problem.

II.
1.) Death in plants. Connected with the Universe.
2.) Death in animals. Connected with Nature.
3.) Death in man. Connected with Earth.

III.
1.) The process of breathing.
   in plants, animal & man.
2.) The development of the blood in animal & man.
3.) The formation of the heart. The Cross.

IV.
1.) The 3 fold nature of man.
   Man in his sense- & nerve-system.
   Man in his metabolic system.
   In the nerves we kill our own life.
   In metabolism we destroy foreign life.
2.) The blood as regulator between life & death.
3.) The heart as creator of Consciousness.
   Fear, anxiety.

V.
1.) The oil-lamp.
   Sleeping, waking.
   Who fills the oil during night?
   Who lits the candle in the morning?
2.) The higher nature of Man's existence.

2. Obituary for Wolfgang Beverley[1]

Our friend has died. He has laid down his physical cloak at an early age and joined the ranks of the unseen. He has crossed the threshold into the land of the dead.

A communal movement like Camphill – to which not only the co-workers, but the children and their parents belong as well as our friends and well-wishers – should consciously face such an event and keep it well in mind. Whenever one of us – child or adult, young or old – has died or will die, a new bond to yonder land over the threshold is established. It connects our work with those friends and strengthens the communion between the two worlds.

A social organism can only grow and unfold when the dead become part of it; when they are consciously considered as helpers and guides in times of stress and joy. As much as a graveyard belongs to our towns and villages, so are the dead (not their corpses but the active entities) part of us, who are still on earth.

Thus Wolfgang is one of us wherever Camphill lives. He should not be forgotten or passed by; he will then become an active entity of great force and power of spiritual strength.

Wolfgang belonged to the stream of curative education long before he was born. His father was a teacher at the Sonnenhof in Arlesheim and Ita Wegman, the head of the curative and medical work there, expected the child to grow up in Arlesheim. She had a room prepared for him and his mother. But things did not happen as expected. The child was born in Germany; he bore the stamp of illegitimacy and spent his childhood in various places. First he lived with his grandparents and later was pushed from pillar to post.

His was the destiny of a homeless and parentless boy. His heart was filled with loneliness. He gained friends and threw them off again. Until at last, when he was sixteen years of age, a good lady – a widow – gave him shelter and care. It was there that he heard of Camphill and immediately joined. His destiny had been waiting for this moment of decision.

I remember his arrival; rough, boisterous, self-assured and yet so tender that anything could make him weep. He was the typical mixture of a youngster who had had to educate himself: a rough and unkempt surface with far too tender a core beneath; a maladjusted boy coming from a defeated country.

Wolfgang adjusted himself to a life of regular work and study with great difficulties. But his heart – full of fire and warmth – helped him to overcome many obstacles. He learned with great zeal and was ready to do any kind of work. He began to love the handicapped children and they taught him to express his own tenderness in meeting others. He managed the training course rather well and entered the group of teachers.

For a time he left Camphill and worked in the Sheiling Schools and later returned. Finally he decided (it was about 1958) to join Botton Village where a number of hidden abilities came to light. He made the first attempt to open a village store. He bought and sold with great understanding for sellers and buyers. His shop made great strides and he established many new connections between the village and a number of firms and tradespeople. He was so successful that he took on the general management of wholesale trading for articles made in the village.

At the same time he achieved the greatest aim of his

life: he started his own family. Solveig became his beloved wife and they had two children, a boy and a girl. He was a devoted husband and a loving father, trying to give to his children what he himself missed as as child.

Then destiny struck. A severe kidney disease set in with high blood pressure. He suffered a great deal of headache, nausea and pain all over his body. He did not believe that death was near. And he had one great wish should he recover – and he was convinced he would – to become a priest. He was eager to preach the gospel and distribute the holy sacrament to those in need.

With this longing Wolfgang parted from the earth. These are the wings which carry him upwards to live in the service of Christ on the other side.

We, who are left behind, are grateful that we were united with him down here. His life was not easy; his way was stony; but his honesty was great and pure. He was one of the many who prepared the steps of Raphael, the healer among human beings: a tradesman in human understanding and interpersonal relationship.

When I think of Wolfgang, I see before me the youth Tobias, who walked at Raphael's side to overcome the powers of evil and find the medicine to heal his father's blindness. He was a true servant of Raphael-Mercurius and we unite with him in the words: *Christus verus Mercurius est.*

APPENDIX

3. Translation of a letter to Tilla Frahm[2]

Tilla Frahm's husband, Ernst Frahm, was priest of the Christian Community in Nürnberg. König had met him at least in 1961 on his visit to Nürnberg and Ansbach, and noted in his diary that he had had a long and interesting conversation with him. In spring of 1963 Tilla Frahm had read Karl König's essays about the thalidomide catastrophe,[3] and contacted him because her husband had died on February 6, 1963.

January 5, 1964

My dear Mrs Frahm

I thank you from my heart for your letter with the detailed description of your husband's illness and death. It really is harrowing to read about the last days of this priest. And yet I am sure that nothing could have saved him. I am deeply convinced that diseases do not cause death, but that death – if it is so determined – will attract the disease that it needs in order to loosen the connection between the soul-spirit and the bodily form.

The circumstances that really do seem to be so detrimentally confused and negative if one sees them from the outside, form a net of connections that made it possible that the soul of your husband could leave the earth just at the time of the great constellation, in order to deliver message of earthly tidings to the Council of the Gods that was taking place. That was what I experienced in reading your letter and this came to me repeatedly in re-reading what you had written about the course of this destiny.

I am very grateful to you for the trust you place in me

and hope that we will be able to meet properly in person before too long.

With my best wishes for the New Year and with heartfelt thanks, I remain

Yours sincerely
Dr Karl König

APPENDIX

4. An excerpt from Karl König's diary[4]

Karl König was staying in Harley Street in London for a few days, as was often the case – he used the house in the famous physicians' street to meet with parents and to see children. From there it was not far to the English Camphill schools in Ringwood and Thornbury, where he visited to give talks and attend meetings. During that time he also used the opportunity to visit Ferdinand Rauter, a musician – pianist and composer – who was also a refugee from Vienna. They had met in internment camp on the Isle of Man in 1940 and Rauter had followed König to Camphill, where he stayed for some time before moving to London in order to take up his musical career again. Rauter died in December 1988. Still today the Ferdinand Rauter Memorial Prize is regularly presented for pianists in London. At the time König was working intensively on questions of music therapy.

April 22, 1953

In the evening I visit Rauters and there I was to meet a Dr Zanker who had evidently started some years ago to include music in the treatment of mentally ill patients. He is a disappointment; a typical man of the last century. He is Jewish and from Vienna, but brings with him all the good-naturedness and foolishness that are to be found there.

Also the Rauters are a disappointment. And the question arises: what distinguishes me from these people and makes me feel so strange and defensive in their presence? And suddenly I realise that their apparent superficiality is caused by the fact that they all continuously forget death, while in me there is a continuous presence of consciousness of death somewhere in the depths of my soul. This state of unison with death creates certitude of spiritual existence.

5. Notes for a lecture on suicide, 1963[5]
Suicide as destiny and the question of reincarnation

I.
1. It could be seen as arrogant to want to cover such an extensive theme as the question of suicide in one single lecture. But that is also not really the intention. Only a few aspects are to be discussed which, in turn, can be instrumental in leading on to more.
2. One could also ask why I want to discuss just this theme of suicide here in the city of Vienna. It is eminently an *Austrian problem*. However one wants to look at it, the Danube area and suicide are closely connected. *Raimund, Stifter, Weininger, Boltzmann* and many more; *Weinheber, Stefan Zweig* ... a never-ending series.
3. Vienna as city of suicides. *Numbers* quote p. 181 (Siegmund). In Germany today suicide stands at 7th place in the death statistics. Just after road deaths. What is suicide?

II
1. When one begins with studies in the phenomena of suicide one also begins to discover the profound extent of the problem. Suicide is not only spread out over the whole world: with indigenous and civilized peoples, in east and west; it is also known from oldest times, and we know of many famous suicides from ancient times. *Socrates, Cato, King Herlang, the young women of Miletus* (Plutarch), *Empedocles*.
2. Points of view about suicide:
Plato quote p. 14 (Siegmund)
Aristotle

APPENDIX

> *Religious sacrificial deaths: Buddhist monks in Vietnam*
> *Jewish suicides*
> *The god Chiron*
> *Saguntum* (Hannibal)
> *Abydos* (Phillip V)

3. In the Old and New Testaments:
   King Saul – desperation
   Samson – revenge (example of the Wotyaks who hanged themselves in the court of their foes)
   Judas – outcast, betrayal, loneliness
   Here we already see various differentiated aspects of the phenomena.

III

1. One cannot grasp the totality of this subject, however, if one tries by methods of usual trains of thought.
   Classifications: *Meininger – Lerchental*
   Quote (p. 3) *Reichardt*
   One stays in superficiality this way. Also *Zilborg's* views are of no help (quote p. 117).
   To see suicide as an illness will lead to our goal.
2. What is it? It is a *phenomena of humanity*.
   The human soul carries the will to suicide within it. Every human being is *potentially suicidal*.
   Everyone has it.
   Many attempt it, in thought or decision.
   Few carry it out.
   Quote: over 700 suicide attempts (p. 121).
3. What triggers this phenomena in the human soul ?
   The human being within itself:
   soul and spirit are struggling with each other;
   soul-spirit and bodily being are struggling with each other.
   Creation and creator
   The human being and God.

The human being and the world are struggling with each other.
The individuality and destiny are struggling with each other.

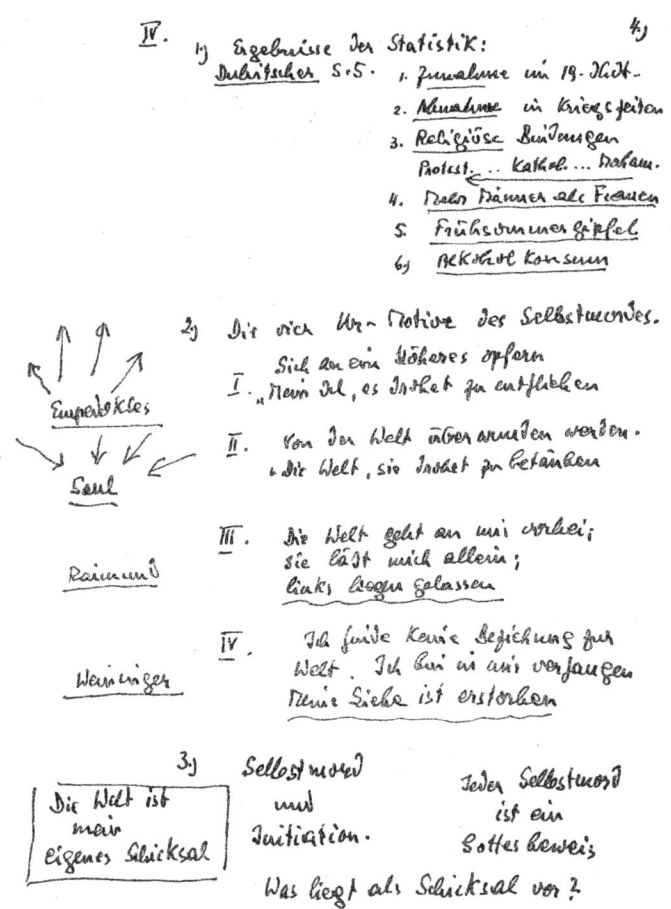

A page of König's notes for this lecture.

IV

1. Results of statistics: (Dubitscher p. 5)
    1. Increase in 19th century
    2. Decrease during wartime
    3. Religious background:
        Protestant – Catholic – Islam
    4. More men than women
    5. Summer peak
    6. Alcohol consumption
2. The four archetypal motives for suicide:
    I. To sacrifice oneself for something higher: 'My self threatens to break away':
        Empedocles
    II. To be overwhelmed by the world: 'The world threatens to stupefy the inborn forces of my soul':
        Saul
    III. The world passes me by, leaves me in solitude by the wayside:
        Raimund
    IV. I find no connection to the world. I am caught up within myself, my love has withered away:
        Weininger
3. The world is my own destiny.
    Suicide and initiation.
    Every suicide is proof of God.
    What kind of destiny is shown?

V

1. If we, however, ask what destiny lies behind a suicide, then it is not anything generic but in every case specific. A *completed* suicide is something different to an *attempt* or, more so, to one that remains a *plan*.

    A *completed* suicide has the influence of forces of destiny.

    In *attempted* suicide destiny is provoked (story of the nephew of Mrs. Neugart)

In *planned* suicide that is not attempted creation is struggling with its creator.
2. *Otto Weininger* April 3, 1880 – October 4, 1903.
Lineage and character.
Domenico [Tommaso] Campanella [Civitas Solis] September 15, 1568 – May 21, 1639.
Imprisoned: August 1599 – May 15, 1626 (27 years)
Weininger's description.
3. *Ferdinand Raimund:* June 1, 1790 – August 29 ... September 5, 1836.
His life, his plays, ghosts, human confusion, Valentin – Aschenmann – Habakuk. Quote: planing song p. 4: Busy are the folks / With quarrelling here – / And death comes past / Just by your leave.
Cruelty to animals, dogs, domestic animals.

V

1. Humankind at the threshold.
Suicide, in its increasing significance is just another sign of this situation.
Human beings cannot escape the need to clarify their connection to God, from whom they have received their destiny.
Either: *suicide*
or: *path of initiation*
And so long you have not experienced this: to die and so to grow ...[6]
No religion can help. The freedom of self-discovery – as creator alone.
2. *Kierkegaard:* Illness leading to death.
Lazarus: 'This illness is not unto to death, it is for the glory of God, so that the Son of God might be glorified by means of it.' (John 11:4)
With this, however, a new chapter begins.

APPENDIX

6. Notes from Karl König's last lecture series, 1966[7]

The gate of the sun and the gate of the moon

I. In yesterday's public lecture, I tried to characterise the problem of euthanasia as it presents itself to humankind today. And it was indeed important to point out that a solution to this problem will only be possible if we take seriously the spiritual questions which humankind is confronted with today. Questions that can be solved if you consider the humanities.

The question of birth and death. Quote from Rudolf Steiner (lecture on Oct 25, 1919, p. 92).

The consciousness soul age.

The confrontation of humanity. Thalidomide disaster, old people, insane, miscarriages.

II. There is a presentation by Rudolf Steiner in which he describes the gate of death and the gate of birth. It is in that important lecture of January 25, 1924 in Bern. The Day of Saint Paul.

There he calls these two gates that of the sun and that of the moon.

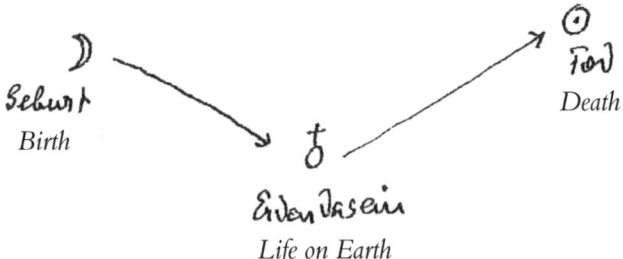
Birth — Life on Earth — Death

Going back to what was presented yesterday, we can now say: Miscarried children gather at the gate of the moon. We must develop the idea that those who do not find their way into life remain too closely and intimately connected to the moon.

The old people, however, want to go towards the sun and cannot reach it. They stand like a mighty cloud in front of this gate of the sun; wanting to pass through, but unable to reach it.

Thus there are the two social phenomena that face us today. The one in front of the gate of the moon; the other in front of the gate of the sun.

What does that mean?

III. It seems like a phrase when today one says that the earth has become whole. And yet it is true; as early as 1912 Rudolf Steiner pointed out this phenomenon.

He characterised the spread of technology spanning the earth with all its consequences for humankind. Quote lecture May 5, 1912 (p. 3).

And it is then clearly pointed out that this body cannot remain alone; that a soul must join it. It complements what would otherwise be left alone. Quote lecture May 5, 1912 (pp. 3f).

But because the expected soul did not come to complement the body, the victims of this unfulfilled complement now wait at the edge of life on earth – standing in front of the moon and the sun – for their redemption.

It is the karma of humankind that confronts us: the children are calling; the old ones are waiting. Christ spreads out his arms and waits for fulfilment.

IV. But now Rudolf Steiner characterises the two goals in a particular way.

The sun: general – human.

APPENDIX

The moon: individual – human.
Quote p. 5. How is this to be understood?
The colony of the moon teachers.
Our individual characteristics.
Quote p. 4. How does this process take place?
The formation of the spirit germ.
Arrival of the soul at the moon.
Earthly germ and spirit germ. The seventeenth day. The formation of the etheric body. The integration of the karma-package. The human being is individualised. If we succeed in doing this to some extent, large parts of the general will remain.
Spirit germ and Down syndrome. The four group souls of humankind, and so on.

V. Rudolf Steiner has however, pointed out another thing in this context. The great metamorphosis between the head and the limbs. This transformation takes place in such a way that the limbs are future-like, Sun-like; they turn into a past-like, moon-like, in the head.
The limbs point to the future. The head points to the past.

Quote pp. 6f. The sun tears us out of our bondage to the earthly. *The old ones.*
The brain and the moon make us selfish. *The miscarried.*
Reincarnation and karma.

113

VI. 'You World Son of the moon ... You World Son of the sun ...' Quote pp. 10f.

The Son of Man who comes in the clouds, and then will appear the sign of the Son of Man in the heavens; and then all the peoples of the earth weep, and will see the Son of man coming in the clouds of the heavens, with power and great glory? [Matt 24:30]

Quote lecture of Jan 25, 1910 (p. 21). (Also on Jan 25, but 14 years before [previously quoted lecture])

'But soon after the tribulation of those days, the sun will be darkened, and the moon will not give its light; the stars will fall from the sky, and the powers of the heavens will be shaken' [Matt 24:29].

VI [VII] The soul is peace. The rose cross. Quote lecture May 5, 1912 (p. 18). Mutual understanding, that is peace.

At the turning point of time ... shepherds' hearts, kings' heads.

APPENDIX

7. Karl König's research into the Calendar of the Soul: the Threshold in the Circle of the Year

Richard Steel

It has always struck me as significant that Karl König began his intensive, life-long studies of the anthroposophical Calendar of the soul in the year 1933, knowing, or sensing – we don't really know which – that this symphony of 52 verses was the right inner work to counterbalance the forces of evil and death that were already closing in like a dark cloud over Central Europe. Rudolf Steiner had given these verses in the years before the First World War, and during the war had a miniature version sent to the front line troops in cigarette packets. König certainly knew that these verses carry a special healing quality – especially in preparing the human being for the encounter with the threshold to the spiritual world; whether the threshold is approached on a path of inner schooling or through death, it is the same threshold.

The metamorphosis of the cross

Karl König discovered quite soon in his studies (seemingly in 1933 already) that the 52 verses of the Calendar of the Soul in their totality have an inner structure – he spoke of 'architecture' – with cosmic reality, like the geometry of the stars. Within this structure the main formative principle is the connection of verses in groups of four, with two pairs of 'opposing' themes. Firstly, for each verse there is the opposite verse, and secondly there is the verse reflected by an equal number of weeks away from Easter, together with its opposite. Thus there is always one verse from each 'quarter' of the festive year. As the Calendar begins with Easter we find a connection from the time after Easter with the time before Easter, and likewise before and after Michaelmas. In this way a cross appears in the circle of the year, which, however, does not keep the same form throughout the year, because the verses belonging together are not always the same distance from each other – it is a dynamic process, a metamorphosis. König discovered this 'pattern' as a key and great help to experiencing the totality of the Calendar of the Soul as a complete work of art. The drawings König made to illustrate this he called the *Metamorphosis of the Cross*.[8]

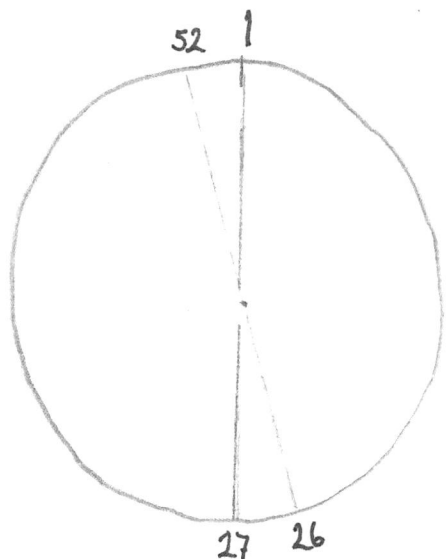

A group of four verses: Easter (1) and opposite Michaelmas (27), the Easter verse is reflected by the verse a week before Easter (52) and its opposite (26).

APPENDIX

But if we see the metamorphosis of this cross from Easter onwards, step by step, by the seventh step the verses become equidistant and so the cross becomes a right-angled cross. In other words, this cross appears four times during the year.

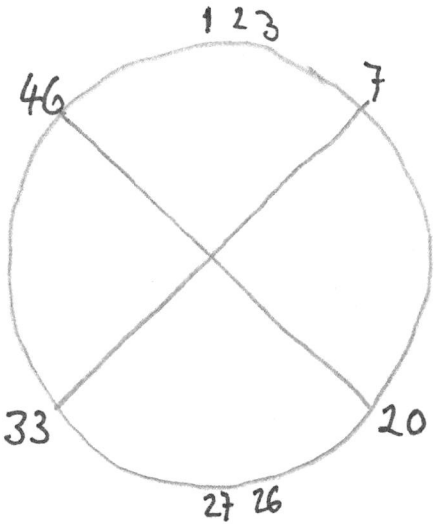

The group of four verses seven weeks after Easter (7) and opposite (33), its reflection (46) seven weeks before Easter and its opposite (20).

One can be in awe of the fact, that it is just here that the only two verses with the theme of death (33 and 20) are connected, being reflections of one another. The other two verses (7 and 46) are similarly threshold verses, giving warning of a kind of death – the threat of breaking away, and the threat of stupefying.

> 7 *May 19–25*
> My self threatens to break away
> Through strong enticement of the light of worlds.
> Now rise, my boding power,
> Assume in strength your rightful throne,

Replace in me the might of thinking
Which in the senses' show
Is like to lose itself

20 *August 18–24*
Now first I feel my being –
Which, torn from world existence,
Within itself must quench the self,
And building on itself alone
Must kill the self-enclosed self.

33 *November 17–23*
Now first I feel the world,
Which, reft of my indwelling soul,
Would as a frozen waste
Unfold its feeble life,
Create itself anew in human souls,
That in itself could look for death alone.

46 *February 16–22*
The world threatens to stupefy
The inborn forces of my soul.
Now rise from spirit depths
In all your radiance, memory.
Establish my beholding,
Which only through the force of will
Can hold itself erect.

APPENDIX

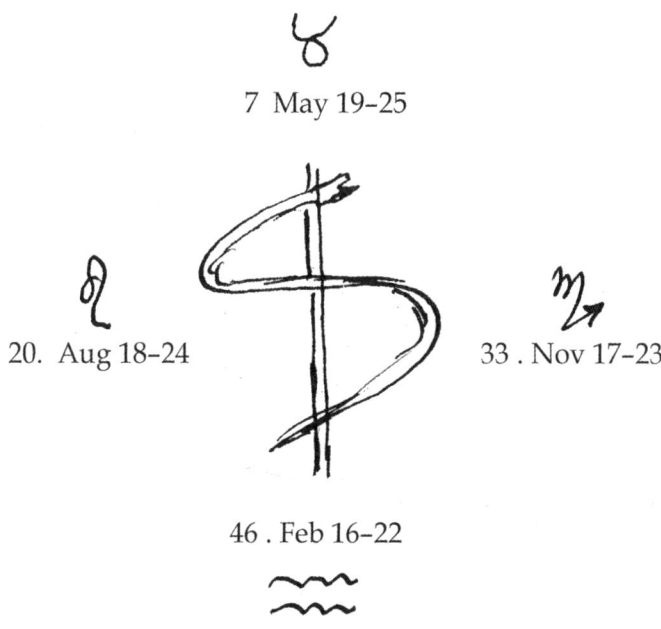

Karl König's final drawing for the seventh cross in the series of 13 (September 1952). From 'The Metamorphosis of the Cross', The Calendar of the Soul: A Commentary.

During his studies König added the name of one of the disciples to each cross – for this cross of death and warning he chose the name Judas. It would, however, be quite in keeping with König's studies to add to Judas the name of Christ to this cross. On the one hand, death, danger and evil can be seen in the figure of Judas, but on the other it is certainly the being of Christ who awaits us and guides us at these threshold situations, and who overcomes the abyss and death itself. König did in fact see the path of the whole Calendar of the Soul leading to the being of Christ:

> The Calendar of the Soul can indeed be seen as a path of initiation that leads into the planetary sphere and thence to the sphere where the etheric Christ lives.[9]

König points out that the rhythm and the changing connections of this cross bring us into a new level of experience within the cycle of the year. Rudolf Steiner gave an indication in this direction a year before he published the Calendar of the Soul, probably out of his preparation of it. Here Steiner suggested that a new connection to time would be necessary – a new calendar. The usual calendars of today are purely abstract; nowadays it would be important to connect to the cosmic dimension of time, which is a living process and engages our own life forces. In this way the spirit can flow into and enliven the soul. Further in the lecture he then described how in the future the Christ impulse will also need to be taken into the soul – this will be the only way for the development of the 'I' to be fruitful. Here he quoted the words of St Paul, 'Not I but Christ in me.'[10]

The seventh verse is a significant threshold on the path of the soul through the year, for it is the threshold between Ascension and Whitsun. However, through Karl König's studies we begin to realise that this cross is in itself a threshold and that each of the verses brings us to the situation of the threshold. Each of these four verses are thresholds between the main festivals of the year. It is a death and transformation in all four cases. For instance, verse 46 is for the week of Carnival, the eve of Passiontide, and is the threshold between Christmas and Easter.

The special place of this one cross within the cycle of the year has to do with the mysteries of numbers too: 52 weeks do not divide into 12 as a cosmic structure might imply, but into 13. From a qualitative viewpoint 13 reflects the mysterious principle of 12 + 1. There are four seasons each of 12 + 1 weeks. Verse 7 stands at the threshold between the spring/Easter weeks and the summer/St John's weeks, verse 20 is the threshold from summer to autumn/Michaelmas, verse 33 is the threshold between Michaelmas

APPENDIX

and winter/Christmas, and verse 46 is at the threshold between Christmas and spring/Easter. It is as if the right-angled cross has withheld itself from the dynamics and life of the yearly rhythms in order to present us with the challenge of death and becoming. Around these pillars of resistance and rigidity the verses of the festivals mirror each other: for instance, after the death experience of verse 20 comes the first Michaelmas verse (21: 'I feel a power unwonted') and before the death experience of verse 33, the last verse of Michaelmas, the transformation ('I feel my proper strength').

Suicide in the cycle of the year

At various times throughout his life Karl König worked with the question of suicide. We know from his accounts of the days in March 1938 as the city of Vienna was overrun by Nazi troops, that many people committed suicide. It seems he was also called out as physician in such cases a number of times. In the 'Autobiographic Fragment' (published in *My Task*) he wrote the following:

> I was often called out as a doctor during these days to attend to suicide cases amongst my patients, they opened gas taps, threw themselves onto the streets from the top floors of their houses, overdosed on morphine or even shot themselves and their families. One despairing act followed another and the 'victors' did everything to intensify fear and confusion.

In the years before he fled from Germany, König had often spoken in courses for nurses and social workers in German cities about social and medical problems and had included the question of suicide, but now in Vienna he was confronted with it at a new level. Towards the end of his life the theme came once more into the foreground as he chose to talk about it during his lecture series in October 1963 in Vienna. The main subject of his lectures was otherwise the twelve senses.

In the weeks leading up to this lecture he of course lived with the preparation for it, and wrote a few entries about it in his diary:

> October 1: I begin to read two books about suicide and it slowly becomes clear to me how extremely wide this phenomenon is. It is a chapter of its own within anthropology. But what is it? The eternal struggle between soul and spirit within the human being ...
>
> October 3: I begin during the morning to write down my thoughts about suicide in a more extensive manner. The four verses of the Calendar of the Soul are a great help with this, as they have to do with the battle between 'I' and world. With this guideline I can work through the four main motifs that lead to suicide. That is a very helpful recognition that has come to me.

It would seem that the preparatory notes in Section 5 of this appendix resulted from these days of study, as well as the note about the four verses (below). The verses led him to the composition of his lecture, and in the notes we find these four verses of the Calendar of the Soul as a fundamental structuring principle for the wide phenomena of suicide.

Before leaving the Lake Constance for Vienna, König went for a first proper visit to Föhrenbühl since the pioneer group had moved there from Brachenreuthe. He is very pleased with the work there and with the beautiful property, remarking in his diary, 'I can almost see what can come about here in the next years.' Then he travelled

APPENDIX

to Stuttgart, because his friend and colleague Eberhard Schickler had died. He chose the names for the first two newly-built houses in the Camphill Schools community in Föhrenbühl as those of his closest friends in the anthroposophical medical movement: Eugen Kolisko and Eberhard Schickler. The old house, which was already standing, he named after Ita Wegman, his beloved mentor and leader of the Medical Section of the Goetheanum, who had died in 1943.

König gave a short address at the memorial service for Schickler and stayed that night as guest of Mrs Schickler. Having slept in Eberhard Schickler's room, König noted the next day in his diary:

> The night was one of the most difficult I have ever experienced. I can feel the waves of his thoughts.

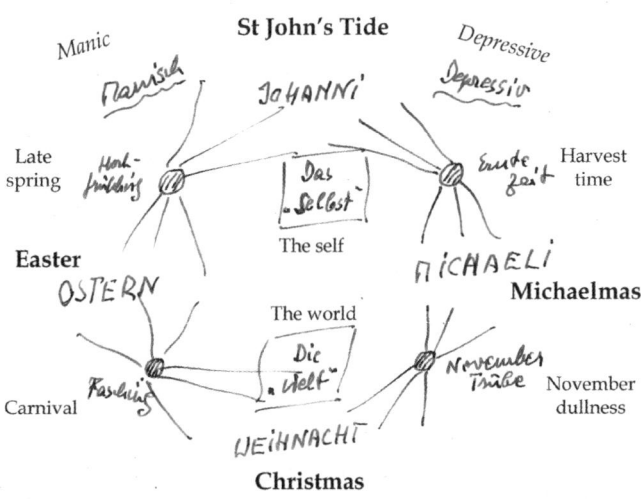

A note from König's lecture preparation, 1963. The four 'points' of the four Calendar of the Soul verses ray out into the circle of the year. The drawing shows them as seasonal 'hotspots' for suicide.

123

On October 13, 1963 he gave the lecture entitled: 'Suicide as a Question of Destiny and Reincarnation.' Unfortunately the lecture was not recorded in any way, but we have König's notes (in Section 5 of this appendix).

At the end of his life, in the last essay he wrote about the background and future aspirations of the Camphill Movement, and of the curative movement altogether, he included the needs of suicidal people:

> The curative educational attitude needs to express itself in all kinds of social work – in pastoral care, in the care for the elderly, in the rehabilitation of mentally ill and physically handicapped people, in the guidance of orphans and refugees, of suicidal and desperate individuals.[11]

Soul death – or 'second death'

Not only the metamorphosis of the cross found artistic expression through Karl König. It was during his internment in 1940, when he was in a special way preparing the inner aspects of what was to become the Camphill movement, that he drew pictures for each verse.[12]

To complete this reflection on König's studies of death within the Calendar of the Soul we should therefore take a look at the pictures for the individual verses in question, particularly at the picture for the August verse (verse 20). Although we have no indications as to the contents of the pictures by Karl König himself, and without wanting to interpret art too strongly that would narrow down the work to mere intellectual symbolics, nevertheless, it is noteworthy how this picture shows the opposite of the natural death processes that are in verse 33 for November. The death process in November is much easier to relate too: who does not know the trials of soul when November comes, daylight recedes and we have to more and more face ourselves? We can easily see – even if it is not always easy to experience – how the human being needs to rise above nature, and *not* die with the dying plant world and the last flash of autumn colour. Therefore the picture for verse 33 is easy to understand and relate to our own experience. It is, however, not so easy to relate death processes to August, and yet verse 20, the 'reflection', is the second verse concerning death. It is an 'inner' death process and certainly of particular significance for our times – we are told that death can be experienced not only by physically leaving this earth, but by leaving our true 'homeland', the spirit. It is the death of the soul itself, and this is strongly expressed by the simple elements of the picture. If our soul is bereft of its connection to the spirit, then it perishes in a twofold way.

The soul is a bridge between worlds, connecting directly on the one hand to the spirit world and on the other to the life forces of the earthly world. It is a task for humanity to cultivate, to ennoble soul life in such a way that it reflects less and less our idiosyncrasies and more of what we can gain from objective spirituality. The soul becomes 'purer' or more translucent – like a crystal that lets the light through in a very special way. If this does not happen then the crystal becomes tarnished, or clouded with 'illusion vain of selfhood' (as it is called in the winter verse, 40). In this case the other side of the bridge – where the soul reaches into the life forces of our own body – can receive no nourishment, no 'water of life' from the sustaining spirit, and our plant-like etheric flow will wither.

In August it is not the 'natural' death that we face, but a step towards the 'second death' or 'soul death' that is described in the Apocalypse of John (20:6, 14). To die away from the spirit world that we also belong to, is a different process than dying from the natural world.

König's drawing for verse 20 of the Calendar of the Soul (from An Inner Journey through the Year *which has the picture in colour).*

Karl König reminds us of a connection between these two verses of death and the words spoken in the Children's Service, as it is the being of Christ standing at these thresholds:

> That leads the living into death that it may live anew;
> That leads what is dead into life that it may behold the spirit.

At Easter we experience death and resurrection. In late summer, when we begin the journey towards Michaelmas, we need to find out of ourselves the forces of resurrection, the reconnection to the spirit, in order to meet death in the right way when November comes and the world is dependent on our vitality and spirituality.

Notes

1. *The Gate of Birth and the Gate of Death*
   1. The Camphill School in Thornbury, near Bristol had begun in 1951.
   2. This could well have been said today, but 1958 was also a culmination of various threads: it was the first serious recession of the postwar world economy; after the Suez crisis the Cold War was at its peak; there was fighting in many places – for instance the war in Algiers had begun, the Cuban revolution and the civil war in the Lebanon; the Hungarian uprising had been crushed and the revolution leaders were in court and were soon to be sentenced to death. But there were also great fears about an atomic catastrophe when it became known that the US was storing atomic missiles in Germany and various accidents had happened in atomic power stations.
   3. According to Rudolf Steiner Kali Yuga began 3101 BC and lasted for 5000 years until AD 1899.
   4. For instance in *The Connection Between the Living and the Dead,* lecture of Oct 24, 1916.
   5. Steiner, *The Mystery of the Trinity,* lecture of Aug 22, 1922.
   6. Steiner describe this in *Dying Earth and Living Cosmos,* lecture of April 1, 1918.
   7. *Gegenwärtiges und Vergangenes im Menschengeiste,* lecture of April 4, 1916.

2. *Bridges to Those who Have Died*
   1. Thor Heyerdahl (1914–2002), a Norwegian anthropologist, became famous in 1947 with his *Kon-Tiki Expedition.* His first Easter Island expedition was in 1955–56, described in *Aku-Aku: Secrets of Easter Island.*
   2. In *According to Matthew,* lecture of Sep 10, 1910, and in *The Gospel of St John and its Relation to the Other Gospels,* lecture of July 7, 1909.

3. *The Path Beyond Death*
   1. Steiner, *Links between the Living and the Dead,* lecture of Oct 10, 1913.

2 Steiner, *The Inner Nature of Man.*
3 Steiner, *The Fifth Gospel,* lecture of Feb 10, 1914.
4 A group indeed formed and worked with these lectures for many years within Camphill internationally, and the consciousness for the significance of these lectures is still carried today by some.

The Death of Adalbert Stifter
Translation by Richard Steel. König was very connected to the Austrian writer Adalbert Stifter (1805–68). He wrote this poem in 1955, the 150th anniversary of Stifter's birth, and also wrote an essay about his life and work (published in *At the Threshold of the Modern Age*). Later in life Stifter's physical and mental health declined and he became seriously ill. In deep depression, he slashed his neck with a razor and died three days later.

Transformation
Translation by Richard Steel. This poem without title was written for Easter 1945. Perhaps 'Transformation' or 'Transformation of the Human Being' could have been the title. Karl König wrote these verses into his diary. The Second World War was still raging and on top of this, a difficult time had begun for König: there were inner trials, partially due to various push-backs to his evolving work locally and from within the Anthroposophical Society. Due to this he had more and more doubts as to the continuation of the work at Camphill Schools. At Michaelmas 1945 König made a decisive move to add strength to the inner striving of the community. Here, once more, as at the time of Ita Wegman's death in 1943, the connection of König and of Camphill to the being of Kaspar Hauser became strongly evident (see also *Becoming Human: A Social Task* and *The Spirit of Camphill*). The questioning peaked, however, during the following year, when many of the very ill children they were looking after had died; this led to his creation of the 'Christmas Story' 1946/47 that centres around those who have died (now published in *Stories, Poems and Meditations,* see also the introduction of this book about the Christmas Story).

4. *The Experience of Birth and Death in Childhood*
This essay was first printed in *The Golden Blade,* 1950.
  1 Quoted by Anthony, *The Child's Discovery of Death,* p. 36.
  2 Anthony, *The Child's Discovery of Death,* p. 55.

5 *The Moment of Death Within the Rhythm of the Day and the Year*
First part translated by Richard Steel, second part (about scarlet fever and diphtheria) by Cornelius Bruhn. This essay was written in 1933 for *Natura,* the journal of the Medical Section of the Anthroposophical Society, edited by Ita Wegman.

NOTES

1 *Münchener medizinische Wochenschrift,* July 22, 1932. (Hagentorn's emphasis).
2 *Münchener medizinische Wochenschrift,* Sep 2, 1932.
3 Steiner, *The Cycle of the Year,* lecture of April 8, 1923.
4 Steiner, *From Comets to Cocaine,* lectures of Oct 24, 1922, Jan 20, 1923.
5 *Münchener medizinische Wochenschrift,* H. 30, 1932.

Appendix

1 From *The Cresset,* journal of the Camphill movement, Michaelmas 1964. Wolfgang's real family name was Beuerle, which he changed when he started his new life in Camphill. He died on April 3, 1964.
2 Translation by Richard Steel.
3 After so many children were born with deformed limbs between 1959 and 1962, there was great public interest in the reasons that pointed to the medical drug thalidomide. The Association of Anthroposophic Physicians in Germany was looking for someone to speak about the problem from the point of view of anthroposophic medicine. Karl König was asked as he had already written three essays for the journal *Die Kommenden* on the theme. The concert hall that was booked for April 18,1963 in Stuttgart was soon sold out and so he had to repeat the lecture on April 19. In June, the three essays were printed as a booklet and translated into English for *The Cresset.* König had an unusual viewpoint for the problem and related the catastrophe to the great constellation of Saturn, Jupiter and Mars in connection to all other planets (except Uranus and Neptune), starting in 1959, with its culmination in February of 1962 and lasting into 1963.
4 Translation by Richard Steel.
5 These notes were for a lecture on October 13, 1963 in Vienna. Translation by Richard Steel.
6 Goethe, *West-Eastern Diwan.*
7 These notes were for two lectures: March 6, 1966 in Mainz and March 10 in Pforzheim. Translated by Cornelius Bruhn.
8 A detailed description is in König, *The Calendar of the Soul.*
9 From an Advent address given in 1947, in König, *The Calendar of the Soul.*
10 Steiner, *Background to the Gospel of St Mark,* lecture of March 7, 1911.
11 In the essay 'The Purpose and Value of Curative-Educational Work' in *The Child with Special Needs.*
12 See *An Inner Journey Through the Year.*

Bibliography

Anthony, Sylvia, *The Child's Discovery of Death,* Kegan Paul, Trench, Trubner, London 1940.
Baumer, Gertrud, *Von der Kindesseele,* Voigtlander, Leipzig (no date).
Dunbar, Helen Flanders, *Emotions and Bodily Changes,* Columbia University Press, New York 1947.
Fordham, Michael, *The Life of Childhood,* Kegan Paul, Trench, Trubner, London 1944.
Hebbel, Friedrich, *Meine Kindheit* (Vol. 9 of complete works).
Heyerdahl, Thor, *Aku-Aku: Secrets of Easter Island,* Allen & Unwin, London 1958.
—, *The Kon-Tiki Expedition: By Raft across the South Seas,* Allen & Unwin, London 1948.
Kanner, Leo, *Child Psychiatry,* Charles Thomas, Baltimore 1942.
Katz, David & Rosa, *Conversations with Children,* London 1936.
König, Karl, *At the Threshold of the Modern Age,* Floris Books 2011
—, *Becoming Human: A Social Task,* Floris Books 2011.
—, *The Calendar of the Soul: A Commentary,* Floris Books 2011.
—, *The Child with Special Needs,* Floris Books 2009.
—, *An Inner Journey Through the Year,* Floris Books 2010.
—, *Karl König: My Task,* Floris Books 2008.
—, *The Spirit of Camphill,* Floris Books 2018.
—, *Stories, Poems and Meditations,* Floris Books 2019.
Kurz, Isolde, *Aus meinem Jugendland,* Tübingen 1918.
Layard, John, *The Lady of the Hare,* Faber & Faber, London 1944.
Mitchell, Sir Arthur, *About Dreaming, Laughing, and Blushing* W. Green & Sons, Edinburgh 1905.
Reichardt, Hans, *Die Früherinnerung,* Carl Marhold, Halle 1926.
Rudder, B. de, *Wetter und Jahreszeit als Krankheitsfaktoren,* Springer, Berlin 1931.
Stanley, H.M. *Autobiography,* Sampton Low, London 1910.
Steiner, Rudolf. Volume Nos refer to the Collected Works (CW), or to the German Gesamtausgabe (GA).
—, *According to Matthew* (CW 123) SteinerBooks, USA 2002.
—, *Background to the Gospel of St Mark* (CW 124) Rudolf Steiner Press, UK 1968.

—, *The Connection Between the Living and the Dead* (CW 168) SteinerBooks, USA 2017.
—, *The Cycle of the Year as a Breathing Process of the Earth* (CW 223) Anthroposophic Press, USA 1984.
—, *Dying Earth and Living Cosmos* (CW 181) Rudolf Steiner Press, UK 2015.
—, *The Fifth Gospel* (CW 148) Rudolf Steiner Press, UK 1985.
—, *From Comets to Cocaine* (CW 348) Rudolf Steiner Press, UK 2000.
—, *Gegenwärtiges und Vergangenes im Menschengeiste* (GA 167) Rudolf Steiner Verlag, Switzerland 1962.
—, *The Gospel of St John and its Relation to the Other Gospels* (CW 112) Anthroposophic Press, USA 1983.
—, *Inner Nature of Man and our Life between Death and Rebirth* (CW 153) Rudolf Steiner Press, UK 2013.
—, *Karmic Relations,* Vol 6 (CW 240) Rudolf Steiner Press, UK 2009.
—, *Knowledge of the Higher Worlds* (CW 10) Rudolf Steiner Press, UK 2004.
—, *Links between the Living and the Dead,* Rudolf Steiner Press, UK 1973.
—, *The Mystery of the Trinity* (CW 214) SteinerBooks, USA 2016.

Index

ancestral memory
— Easter Island 34f
— Shinto 27
angel permeates 29
Atlantis 20f

blood 76f
— as realm of unconscious 78
— soul dies into 81f

Calendar of the Soul 115–27
Christ 119f

death
—, looking back on 41
— in the yearly rhythm 92–95

ether body 50f
— Christ-impulse 51
— image of the Holy Shroud 51

fairy tales
— *Green Snake and the Beautiful Lily* 49f
— *Hansel and Gretel* 83
Fall, the 75, 91
fear 74f, 82, 88f

'I'
— fixed after death 41, 47f
— permeated by angel 29

Judas 119

Kali Yuga 21f

language of the dead,
— anthroposophy as 28
— no national character 36f
— verbs 38
life-spirit 29, 47–49
loss of value
— disposable culture 24
— of existance 24
— human lives 23

moon, as gate of birth 42, 111–14

nervous system 76f
— as shield of conciousness 78
— soul reawakens 82

reincarnation
— head/body metamorphosis 38f
— chest/limbs metamorphosis 40f

second death 124f
shame 74f, 82, 89f
spirit-man 29, 47–49
spirit-self 29, 47–49
suicide 106–10
sun, as gate of death 42, 111–14

Karl König's collected works are being published in English by Floris Books and in German by Verlag Freies Geistesleben. They are issued by the Karl König Archive in co-operation with the Ita Wegman Institute for Basic Research into Anthroposophy. They encompass the entire, wide-ranging literary estate of Karl König, including his books, essays, manuscripts, lectures, diaries, notebooks, his extensive correspondence and his artistic works, across twelve subjects.

Karl König Archive subjects

Medicine and study of the human being
Curative education and social therapy
Psychology and education
Agriculture and science
Social questions
The Camphill movement
Christianity and the festivals
Anthroposophy
Spiritual development
History and biographies
Artistic and literary works
Karl König's biography

Karl König Archive
www.karlkoeniginstitute.org
office@karlkoeniginstitute.org

Ita Wegman Institute for Basic Research into Anthroposophy
www.wegmaninstitut.ch
koenigarchiv@wegmaninstitut.ch

For news on all our **latest books**,
and to receive **exclusive discounts**,
join our mailing list at:

florisbooks.co.uk

Plus subscribers get a FREE book
with every online order!

We will never pass your details to anyone else.